CREATING A CLIMATE FOR LEARNING

STRATEGIES TO RAISE ACHIEVEMENT

AT KEY STAGE 2

Rachel Brooks • Laura Sukhnandan • Nicola Flanagan • Caroline Sharp

INVESTOR IN PEOPLE

nfer

Published in July 1999
by the National Foundation for Educational Research
The Mere, Upton Park, Slough, Berkshire, SL1 2DQ

About the NFER

The National Foundation for Educational Research (NFER) is Britain's leading educational research organisation. It is an independent Foundation, undertaking research on behalf of NFER's members (the English and Welsh local authorities and the major professional associations) as well as for external sponsors. Its purpose is to gather, analyse and disseminate research-based information in order to improve education and training. Its staff have a range of experience and expertise spanning all sectors of education from pre-school and primary to further and higher education. The NFER's publications are produced on a not-for-profit basis.

About the Authors

Rachel Brooks is a Research Officer at the NFER. Her previous work has included two studies on the use of information and communications technology (ICT): one on its use in initial teacher training; and the other looking at its application for pupils with special educational needs.

Laura Sukhnandan is also a Research Officer. She has recently completed a literature review on ability grouping and is currently working on a project investigating strategies for addressing gender differences in achievement at primary and secondary level.

Nicola Flanagan was attached to this project as part of a year-long work placement, while studying for a degree in Applied Sociology and Psychology at Surrey University. She also worked on another project during her time at NFER, which entailed a survey of reading intervention schemes designed to help slow readers.

Caroline Sharp is an experienced Senior Research Officer. She has undertaken numerous research studies, many of which have focused on primary schools. Her work includes several studies into issues in early childhood education, research into the effects of the arts on children's learning, and investigations into the contribution of homework and study support.

Contents

Acknowledgements

We would like to take this opportunity to thank our sponsors and everyone who helped in the research. In particular, we would like to thank the LEA advisers who responded to our request for information, and all the schools we contacted to find out more about their strategies. We are particularly grateful to the heads, teachers, pupils and others in the case-study schools who took the time to talk to us about their initiatives. We would like to thank our advisory group members and everyone who commented on the first draft. Finally, we would like to express our gratitude to Mrs Bigland, who let us pilot our observation schedules in her school; to our project secretary, Effie de Souza-Sudell; to David Upton for technical editing and to our colleagues in the NFER library.

Key Issues for Key Stage 2

Primary schools have rarely been under so much pressure to raise achievement since the Victorian system of 'payment by results'. The Government has set ambitious targets for the performance of children in National Curriculum assessments at KS2 (GB. DfEE, 1997). By 2002 at least 80 per cent of 11-year-olds will be expected to reach Level 4 in English and at least 75 per cent should reach the same standard in mathematics. In Wales, the equivalent targets are for between 70 and 80 per cent of 11-year-olds to achieve Level 4 in each of English, mathematics, science and Welsh.

In 1998, the targets were still some way off. The national results for England showed that 65 per cent of children achieved Level 4 or above in English and 59 per cent achieved Level 4 or above in mathematics (QCA, 1998b). In Wales, the proportion of children achieving Level 4 or above were: 64 per cent in English, 61 per cent in mathematics, 69 per cent in science and 65 per cent in Welsh (GB. Welsh Office, 1998).

Evidence from OFSTED inspections has highlighted particular issues for schools at Key Stage 2. The 1996/97 Annual Report (OFSTED, 1998b) identified 'substantial underachievement' at Key Stage 2 in one in eight schools. The report recommended that schools should pay particular attention to Years 3 and 4, where progress was found to be weakest. Although the report for 1997/8 found evidence of some improvement, the Chief Inspector considered that there was still a need for primary schools to prioritise raising standards for children of this age-group (OFSTED, 1999a).

In terms of subject areas, there are particular concerns about standards in information technology, where one in five English schools is failing to comply with National Curriculum requirements (OFSTED, 1998c, 1999a). A recent international study of achievement in mathematics and science (Harris *et al.*, 1997) provided evidence of how English children are performing in relation to those in over 40 countries. The results showed that English nine-year-olds were achieving relatively well in science but poorly in mathematics.

Another issue of concern, in this country as elsewhere, is gender-related patterns of performance. The national results for England show that although 11-year-old boys achieve at virtually the same levels as girls in mathematics and science, there is a substantial gender gap in English. In 1998, only 57 per cent of boys achieved Level 4 or above in English, compared with 73 per cent of girls (QCA, 1998b). There are similar gender-related patterns in Wales, where there is evidence of boys doing less well than girls in both English and Welsh. (The gap between the proportion of boys and girls achieving Level 4 was 18 per cent in English and 13 per cent in Welsh.)

Other important issues in underachievement relate to social deprivation and ethnicity. The 1999 Annual Report from OFSTED shows that primary schools with a high proportion of children eligible for free school meals tend to have poorer achievement, but there is also a large variation in attainment between schools with similar intakes (OFSTED, 1999a).

Analyses of the relationships between ethnicity and performance provide a complex picture (Gillborn and Gipps, 1996; OFSTED, 1999a and b). Children from Black African, Indian and Chinese backgrounds achieve well at primary school relative to children from other ethnic groups. The evidence on the achievement of Black Caribbean children indicates that they achieve in line with national averages, although they are under-represented in the higher levels of achievement at the end of Key Stages 1 and 2. Children from Pakistani and Bangladeshi backgrounds do poorly in the early years, but make better progress as they become more proficient in spoken English. However, the performance of Pakistani and Bangladeshi primary school pupils remains below that of other groups. Gypsy Traveller children are particularly at risk of underachievement at school. There are also important inter-relationships between the influences of ethnicity, gender and social class on educational achievement, as Gillborn and Gipps (1996) point out.

This book highlights some of the strategies schools are using to raise achievement at Key Stage 2. There are examples of national, local and school-based initiatives aimed at raising achievement in a variety of subject areas. There are also examples of strategies targeted at specific groups of pupils. But primary teachers have always been concerned with broader issues than simply improving test results. This is reflected by the inclusion of initiatives to improve children's self-esteem, develop interpersonal skills, improve behaviour and enhance children's motivation to learn. We hope this book will be of interest and practical use to heads, teachers and others concerned with improving the quality of children's learning in primary schools.

Caroline Sharp, 1999

References

GILLBORN, D. and GIPPS, C. (1996). *Recent Research on the Achievements of Ethnic Minority Pupils* (OFSTED Reviews of Research). London: HMSO.

GREAT BRITAIN. DEPARTMENT FOR EDUCATION AND EMPLOYMENT (1997). *Blunkett Sets Tough New Targets* (Press Notice 96/97). London: DfEE.

GREAT BRITAIN. WELSH OFFICE (1998). *National Curriculum Assessment Results in Wales: 1998. Key Stage 2.* Cardiff: Welsh Office, Education Department.

HARRIS, S., KEYS, W. and FERNANDES, C. (1997). *Third International Mathematics and Science Study, Second National Report. Part 1: Achievement in Mathematics and Science at Age 9 in England.* Slough: NFER.

OFFICE FOR STANDARDS IN EDUCATION (1998b). *Standards in the Primary Curriculum 1996-97.* London: OFSTED.

OFFICE FOR STANDARDS IN EDUCATION (1998c). *The Annual Report of Her Majesty's Chief Inspector of Schools: Standards and Quality in Education 1996/97.* London: OFSTED.

OFFICE FOR STANDARDS IN EDUCATION (1999a). *The Annual Report of Her Majesty's Chief Inspector of Schools: Standards and Quality in Education 1997/98.* London: OFSTED.

OFFICE FOR STANDARDS IN EDUCATION (1999b). *Raising the Attainment of Minority Ethnic Pupils: School and LEA Responses.* London: OFSTED.

QUALIFICATIONS AND CURRICULUM AUTHORITY (1998b). *Standards at Key Stage 2: English, Mathematics and Science. Report on the 1998 National Curriculum Assessments for 11-year-olds. A Report for Headteachers, Teachers and Assessment Coordinators.* London: QCA.

About This Book

This book is based on research into strategies used by schools to raise achievement at Key Stage 2. The work was carried out by a team of researchers at the National Foundation for Educational Research.

The aim of this book is to share examples of strategies which schools have found useful in creating a positive climate for learning at Key Stage 2. The book is intended as a resource for heads, governors and teachers looking for ideas and sources of advice. It consists of a series of case-study examples and a set of practical resources.

The case studies

This part of the book features descriptions of 12 schools, all of which have implemented strategies to raise achievement for children in KS2. The strategies range from involvement in national projects to locally based initiatives.

The case studies follow a similar structure. They begin with an introduction describing the school, explaining the context for the initiative and setting out the issues the school was seeking to address. This is followed by a description of the strategy: how it came about, what happened, how long it took and what resources were needed. The next section reflects on the success of the strategy, highlighting what has been achieved, and explaining any adjustments that the school has made. The case studies conclude with a section summarising the advantages (and disadvantages) of the strategies for all involved. We have also included suggestions for further reading, linked to each strategy.

We should point out that although LEA advisers and schools identified these as successful strategies, their impact on children's achievement has sometimes been difficult to judge in 'concrete' terms. This is because some strategies do not easily lend themselves to evaluation, and/or because the schools' procedures for evaluating the initiatives have only recently been put in place. In some cases, the schools introduced several strategies during the same period, so it was difficult to disentangle the relative contribution of each to any improvement in assessment results. In order to strengthen the evidence-base of the book we have reported the findings of related research, where we are aware that such research evidence exists.

Although the case studies describe a diverse range of initiatives, we have attempted to organise them thematically in relation to the particular issues they address. The first three concern specific curriculum initiatives in information technology and mathematics, one of which focused on the needs of children for whom English is an additional language. This is followed by an example of one school's approach to subject specialist teaching. The next three case studies provide descriptions of initiatives aimed at particular groups of children (namely high achievers and boys). The final group of case studies concern strategies aimed at a variety of issues, such as: improving children's personal and evaluation skills; involving parents and volunteers in supporting children's learning; and providing facilities for homework.

Please note that all the schools have been given pseudonyms. A list of participating schools is provided in the appendix.

Resources

Based on the experiences of the people we spoke to, the **Planning Guide** is designed to help schools to develop strategies of their own. A series of questions leads readers through the process of diagnosing areas for development, selecting an appropriate strategy and planning how to put it into practice.

Each case study ends with a selection of related books and videos. These are listed and described in a **Further Reading** section at the end of the book.

The **Appendix** contains a short section describing the research project that formed the basis for the book, together with a list of our advisory group members, the people who commented on the draft version and the 12 case-study schools.

Using Information Technology Across the Curriculum

Peareswood Junior School has invested in information technology (IT) to develop children's IT skills and as a means of raising levels of achievement across the curriculum.

Introduction

As we move towards increased use of information technology at work and in society as a whole, there is a need to equip children with the skills to use IT effectively. Although most primary-age children have access to some IT equipment at school, resources are limited. Recent OFSTED reports have drawn attention to less than satisfactory standards of achievement in IT, particularly at Key Stage 2 (OFSTED, 1998b, 1998c, 1999a). Teachers often lack training and are not confident in teaching IT, and it can be difficult for them to keep up to date with the rapid pace of development in the area.

About the school

Peareswood Junior School is located on the outskirts of a city. Most of the children transfer to the school from a neighbouring infant school. There are 270 children on roll, about 30 per cent of whom are eligible for free school meals. A high proportion of the children come from Asian backgrounds and over a third speak English as an additional language. Fifteen per cent of the children have been identified as having special educational needs. There are two classes in each of four year groups (Year 3–Year 6). The school employs ten full-time teachers and two language support teachers.

The development of the strategy

Information technology was first introduced in the school in 1981 as part of a national initiative, which allocated one computer to every primary school. Since then the school has had a succession of headteachers who have prioritised IT. In 1988, Peareswood was one of two schools selected to participate in an LEA initiative evaluating the potential of computer networks in primary schools. The LEA provided the school with four additional computers, which were networked together. By the early 1990s, when the current head started at the school, there was a computer in each classroom and the school had created a distinct area specifically for IT. The current head has a particular interest in the role of IT, and works with the deputy (who is also the IT coordinator) to update and develop the school's IT facilities.

The strategy

At the time of our visit, the school had approximately 30 computers, all of which were networked together. Children have access to a wide range of programs such as word processing, spreadsheets, mathematics and language programs, desktop publishing and graphics. Each child has his or her own user identification so that they can save their work centrally, regardless of the computer terminal they are using.

We observed an IT lesson led by a Year 3 teacher, supported by the IT coordinator. The purpose of the lesson was to introduce children to a new system and to use a program for making graphs. The 31 children sat at one of the computer terminals with their 'partners' (the teacher had created mixed-ability pairs by grouping a child of higher attainment with a lower-attaining child). The teacher began by drawing the children's attention to the new screen saver and asking children to explain its purpose. She then demonstrated how to log on to the new system, using the TV screen to demonstrate the procedure. The children all followed the instructions, typing in their ID numbers and using the mouse to access the program.

The children had brought with them the results of a survey they had carried out on the numbers of different coloured sweets they had found in packets of *Smarties*. The teacher demonstrated how to input data and how to construct different types of graphs. She also showed them how to alter the colours. The children were then free to construct their own graphs while the teachers circulated to those needing help.

The children worked steadily throughout the lesson. Most seemed to be able to attempt the task with minimal help, although some were initially 'thrown' by the fact that the program did not offer orange as a colour choice. By the end of the lesson, all the pairs had inputted their data, added a title and experimented with different forms of presentation, and most had printed off their results. They had also learned to log on to and off from the new system. The children appeared to enjoy the lesson and were proud of their printed graphs.

The computer area is an open-plan space equipped with 17 computer workstations together with two servers and several printers. There is a desk for the teacher, a white board and a large screen monitor, which can be used to relay the teacher's computer screen display to the class. Every class is timetabled to use the computer area for an hour a week. The IT coordinator teaches four of the classes (one of the two classes in each year group) and the teachers of the remaining four take their own classes for IT.

In addition to this hourly session, children use computers wherever appropriate during their class lessons. Children can leave the classroom to work in the computer area, with permission from their class teachers. The school has given thought to the safety of the children using the computers: the computer area is overlooked by adjacent classrooms and the equipment is permanently clamped in place. Teachers visit the computer area from time to time to supervise the children working there. The children use the computers either to follow up the work which has been done during the hour-long IT session or to use one of the programs designed to support their development in a wide range of different areas such as reading, spelling and mathematics.

The school holds regular open evenings, during which parents are invited to discuss their children's work. The computer network is set up so that children can show their parents the work they've been doing in IT.

The school's IT system is funded solely through the school budget. The head explained that this has been achieved through 'prudent housekeeping and budget management'. Every year approximately £7,000 is put aside for IT, £4,000 of which pays for the leasing of the equipment. The remaining £3,000 is used to purchase new resources, such as software or memory, and to send the IT coordinator on relevant courses. Maintenance and insurance of the equipment is arranged through the LEA.

It's fun because you're learning something.

By leasing, rather than buying their equipment, the school is able to upgrade its hardware every four to five years and thus keep up to date with the latest technological developments. Although the IT resources represent a large financial commitment, the head pointed out that because staff have access to such a comprehensive IT system, they are able to offset some of the costs by designing their own documentation (such as worksheets, booklets, and the school prospectus).

Is it successful?

Teachers identified a number of benefits from their school's investment in IT. These included the development of children's IT and study skills, and the positive effects on children's motivation — all of which have a positive impact on achievement across the curriculum.

Within IT, children develop a range of skills, including the operation of the mouse and computer keyboard, and the ability to access a wide range of programs with confidence. Study skills are fostered, because children learn how to search for relevant material from a number of sources, and to select and integrate it into their work.

However, one of the greatest benefits of the school's IT facilities, as teachers and children pointed out, was its effect on children's enthusiasm and motivation to learn. One teacher commented: *'Children find it exciting so their motivation level is high. They look forward to Wednesday afternoons: they say "Is it computers this afternoon?".'* The Year 5 children we spoke to agreed. One said: *'It's the best lesson, because you get to do loads of games and I love typing.'* Another added: *'It's fun because you're learning something.'*

Teachers pointed out that computer work helps to motivate lower-attaining pupils in particular. These children are able to produce work to a high standard with the aid of computer programs: they are not handicapped by poor handwriting or an inability to spell. By using some of the diagnostic computer learning packages, children get immediate feedback on their work, and can move on to another task designed to reinforce their learning. (Some children find it easier to accept feedback on their progress from a computer program, rather than from their teacher.) Staff also felt that the language programs were helpful for children with English as an additional language, providing options such as a wordbank, spellchecker, thesaurus and help with pronunciation.

Staff felt that the main benefit of IT for them was that it provided an additional means of presenting material and reinforcing teaching. For example one teacher said: *'It's given me a lot more strategies, another tool by which to get things across to the children.'* However, they pointed out that it is important to remember that IT is not a replacement for a teacher and that lessons still had to be carefully planned, led and structured. They also recognised the need to focus separately on children's handwriting and spelling skills, which are not necessarily developed through the use of computers.

Staff felt that their strategy has had a positive impact on the children's achievement. Teachers in the local high school have reported that children from Peareswood are well ahead of children from other junior schools in terms of their IT skills, and the school's 1995 OFSTED inspection noted that the children's IT skills are of a high standard: *'Pupils achieve good standards in the use of information technology and use the equipment confidently'.*

It's given me a lot more strategies, another tool by which to get things across to the children.

The school's assessment scores show steady improvements over a number of years. Comparing the progress of children between KS1 and KS2, the children's 1988 National Curriculum assessment results showed that 14 per cent had increased their attainment by one Level, 62 per cent had gained two Levels and 15 per cent had

gained three Levels. However, staff acknowledged that it is very difficult to assess the specific impact of IT on levels of achievement because it has become embedded throughout the curriculum over a long period of time.

What makes it work?

The use of information technology has been integrated into the school's key stage plans for the last five years. The plan covers all subjects and is reviewed and updated annually. The plan for IT is based on guidance produced by the School Curriculum and Assessment Authority (SCAA, 1997), adapted to meet the needs of the school. It ensures that IT is used to support children's work in as many subjects as possible, and enables teachers to plan for progression in IT skills as children move through the school, providing targets for achievement in IT by the end of KS2.

Summarising their approach, the head said: *'Instead of IT being "subject IT", we actually use it to raise achievement within subject areas. We were able to purchase software so the children could start off on a very simple level in Year 3 and then move up year by year so by the time they get to Year 6 they're using full-blown Word 6.'*

The IT coordinator plays a key role in training and development. In order to fulfil his responsibilities as deputy head and special needs coordinator

as well as IT coordinator, he does not have responsibility for teaching a class of children. This means that he is able to attend relevant courses to keep up to date with the latest educational programs and equipment. He shares information with colleagues during weekly staff meetings and organises special INSET sessions whenever a new program or piece of equipment is introduced to the school. He also provides staff with support and advice on a more informal basis, helping teachers to plan lessons or solve particular problems. As one teacher explained: *'I tell the IT coordinator what I want to teach and he shows me what program would be appropriate and we go through it prior to the lesson.'*

Over the past few years, the staff have changed their approach to teaching IT. When the school expanded its use of IT during the LEA initiative, all the teachers were given responsibility for teaching the area to their own classes. However, this was found

to be very demanding, particularly on people who felt they had less of a flair for the subject. The coordinator explained: *'We decided that the best compromise was that I try and do about 50 per cent of the IT in the school, and the other 50 per cent is done by those people who feel confident to do it.'* Because the IT coordinator takes one class in each Year group, he is able to achieve an overview of children's progress, and to support the teacher of the parallel class.

Postscript

Since our visit, the school has expanded its IT facilities. In addition to 33 computer stations on an existing network, the school has invested in a new 20-station multimedia network and a cabling system which will enable more terminals to be added in future. The new network provides access to the Internet. The school is also involved in a national pilot project which enables children to access multimedia resources via satellite.

Main advantages of this strategy

For pupils

- Children enjoy using IT in their work.

- The investment in IT allows the children to produce highly polished work, incorporating a wide range of different types of presentation (e.g. text, graphs, and pictures).

- Children gain the necessary skills and confidence to use computers as a learning tool.

- Children develop their study skills. They have instant access to a wide range of information sources.

- Diagnostic programs help children to practice and develop their basic literacy and numeracy skills.

- Children with English as an additional language benefit from computer programs that provide assistance with language skills.

- Lower-attaining children can produce work to a high standard of presentation, and are not held back by poor handwriting and spelling.

For teachers

- IT provides staff with an additional tool for teaching across the curriculum.

- Children are well motivated in lessons involving IT.

- Staff receive regular training and support. Their own confidence in using IT has improved.

For parents

- Parents are pleased that the school is helping their children to use IT as an educational tool and are impressed by their children's ability to use IT.

For the school

- The school has built up good computer facilities and equipment.

- The IT facilities are used to produce learning materials and the school prospectus to a high standard of presentation.

- The school's interest in IT was rewarded when it was selected as one of two primary schools to take part in an LEA initiative. The school's IT work received positive recognition in their OFSTED inspection report.

Main disadvantages

- IT is a relatively expensive item, requiring annual expenditure.

References

OFFICE FOR STANDARDS IN EDUCATION (1998b). *The Annual Report of Her Majesty's Chief Inspector of Schools: Standards and Quality in Education 1996/97.* London: OFSTED.

OFFICE FOR STANDARDS IN EDUCATION (1998c). *Standards in the Primary Curriculum 1996–97.* London: OFSTED.

OFFICE FOR STANDARDS IN EDUCATION (1999a). *The Annual Report of Her Majesty's Chief Inspector of Schools: Standards and Quality in Education 1997/98.* London: OFSTED.

SCHOOL CURRICULUM AND ASSESSMENT AUTHORITY (1997). *Expectations in Information Technology at Key Stages 1 and 2.* London: SCAA.

Further reading on Information Technology

CROMPTON, R. and MANN, P. (Eds) (1996). *IT Across the Primary Curriculum.* London: Cassell.

HARRISON, M. (1998). *Coordinating Information and Communications Technology Across the Primary School.* London: Falmer Press.

SCHOOL CURRICULUM AND ASSESSMENT AUTHORITY (1997). *Expectations in Information Technology at Key Stages 1 and 2.* London: SCAA.

Taking Part in the National Numeracy Project and Setting By Ability

Croxley JMI has introduced two strategies aimed at improving achievement in mathematics. The school took part in the pilot of the National Numeracy Project (NNP). At the same time, the school introduced setting in mathematics across Years 3 and 4 and Years 5 and 6.

Introduction

In recent years there has been growing evidence that the performance of English pupils in certain aspects of mathematics lags behind that of many of their international counterparts. This has led to the development of the Numeracy Project, which aims to raise standards in mathematics (Numeracy Task Force, 1998; Reynolds and Muijs, 1999). It is hoped that this will enable the Government to meet its national target for numeracy, which states that 75 per cent of all 11-year-olds should achieve the standard expected for their age by the year 2002.

Setting by ability is becoming increasingly popular in mathematics, particularly in Years 5 and 6 (OFSTED, 1998a). However, two recent reviews of research have concluded that setting is not necessarily an effective method for raising achievement in primary schools (Harlen and Malcolm, 1997; Sukhnandan with Lee, 1998).

About the school

Croxley Juniors and Infants is situated in a mining town in the north of England. The majority of pupils come from white, working-class families and the area suffers from relatively high unemployment. About a quarter of the children are eligible for free school meals.

Twelve years ago, the local junior school and infant school were combined to create the current primary school. There are 214 children on roll, in eight classes from reception to Year 6. Several classes contain mixed-age groups and these are adjusted each year in relation to the intake, so that class sizes are kept to a limit of around 30 children.

The development of the strategy

As a result of an OFSTED inspection in 1994, it became apparent that the mathematics scheme that the school had been using did not cover the requirements of the National Curriculum. The head recognised that staff were very reliant on their existing scheme of work and lacked confidence in teaching mathematics. In order to address these issues, staff decided to devise their own mathematics scheme. About a year later, the head was informed that the National Numeracy Project was to be piloted in their LEA. Having

obtained the support of the staff, she applied to take part in the pilot and the application was accepted in the summer of 1996. The head felt that this provided the school with a welcome opportunity to address their need to develop mathematics teaching and learning.

The school received £600 from the NNP and raised matched funding from the school budget and from the Grants for Educational Support and Training (GEST) scheme. The money was used to provide supply cover for teachers during training and to purchase new mathematics teaching resources.

Before the NNP was introduced, the mathematics coordinator and the key stage 2 link teacher both attended a one-week training course about the NNP. They were introduced to the Project and given help on how to turn the framework into lesson plans and how to introduce the new lesson structure. When they returned from the course, these teachers disseminated the information to the rest of the staff. An NNP consultant provided all staff with six hours of training in preparation for the project, and visited each term for two years to evaluate the project and to provide demonstration lessons, particularly for new staff.

Because of the Project's emphasis on hands-on activities, the school has had to reorganise their existing mathematics resources and purchase new items, such as overhead projectors, board games and 'show me' cards. The school also made changes to the timetable to enable setting to take place across the year-groups, and teachers adapted their planning documents to take account of the new strategy.

Delivery of the NNP began in February 1997 for the whole of the school. Parents received a letter about the new approach to numeracy and a meeting was held to discuss the initiative with parents. In September, two KS2 teachers took part in training to help them develop their interactive skills still further.

The strategy

Staff decided to implement setting for mathematics by combining Year 5 with 6 and Year 3 with 4

and dividing each group into one higher- and one lower-ability group. The head felt that this was necessary in order to reduce the wide range of ability within each class and to enable a more rapid pace of delivery. Pupils were allocated to mathematics sets in September. In order to ensure that the work is at an appropriate level, these groupings were reviewed in October and again each term.

Each day children in KS2 receive a 50-minute session focusing on numeracy. The lessons follow the numeracy framework in terms of objectives and structure. During the first ten minutes the whole class works on mental maths, the following 30 minutes are spent on the main activity where pupils can work individually, in ability groups or as a whole class, and the final ten minutes consist of a plenary session with the whole class.

Is it successful?

The teachers we spoke to said they welcomed the Numeracy Framework. One teacher commented on the way it had improved pupils' motivation: *'It's given our school a real buzz to do maths. We'll say "It's maths", and it's "Yes!", and it's lovely to get that reaction from them.'*

It's given our school a real buzz to do maths.

In particular, teachers felt that the highly structured format had enabled them to teach mathematics much more effectively, because it ensured that all topics were covered comprehensively. Teachers also pointed out that the emphasis on

---

We observed one numeracy lesson with a mixed Year 5 and 6 higher-ability group. At the beginning of the lesson, the teacher explained that they were going to start by looking at doubling and halving. Children were given cards with problems written on them, and the teacher started a stopwatch. The first mental arithmetic problem was 'double 17'. The child with the number 34 at the top of their card called out the answer, and then asked the next question printed on the card: 'half 76'. The children managed to complete their questions within two minutes and 35 seconds — the fastest to date.

The main part of the lesson consisted of 30 minutes on decimals, starting with easy problems. For example, the teacher asked pupils to show her the decimal on their cards that represented six-tenths. This progressed to asking more complex questions (such as 'double 3.5' and 'halve 8.6'). For the majority of this time, the teacher taught

from the front of the class. Throughout the 30 minutes, she gave the children timed activities to complete, either on their own or in pairs, and the children continually fed back their findings to the whole class. The teacher used an overhead projector to ask children to identify a decimal that would come between two adjacent numbers. In the final ten minutes there was a question-and-answer session in which the children summarised what they had learned during the lesson.

The structure of the lesson appeared to keep the children fully involved and the rapid pace kept the children's attention focused on their tasks. The lesson promoted a high level of interaction between pupils and teachers, and the use of games, together with the rapid pace, meant that children had little opportunity to become bored. The children appeared to be challenged by the level of work, and most were able to complete their tasks within the allotted time.

direct teaching and interactive oral work was rewarding and enabled them to have a better grasp of pupils' progress. As one teacher explained: *'We are more involved in teaching, we are actually teaching rather than managing children with maths books ... we are more aware of who is understanding and who isn't.'*

The games help us to understand and make maths more fun.

Furthermore, staff believed that the Numeracy Framework had helped to increase their confidence in teaching mathematics. As one teacher said: *'Teachers are being allowed to teach and use the skills for which they were trained ... they feel like they are in control.'*

The children we spoke to felt that the new structure and content were a great improvement on previous mathematics lessons. One pupil, reflecting on previous mathematics lessons, commented: *'It was pretty boring 'cos if you were stuck on an answer you'd have to put your hand up and wait about five minutes 'cos everyone was stuck.'* Pupils welcomed the faster pace and improved feedback in the new lessons. Their enjoyment of maths had increased greatly. As one boy said: *'The games help us to understand and make maths more fun'.* Another added: *'The games are mega!'*

Pupils of all abilities responded well to the idea of setting by ability: *'It's better if it makes you learn. It's a different teacher and different people around you so that's good.'*

Since the introduction of the NNP, the school has received positive feedback about their mathematics teaching from a visiting HMI. Staff feel that there is informal evidence that the NNP is having a positive impact on children's mathematics skills. One teacher said: *'There's a general feeling that their [the children's] mental skills are being sharpened up considerably; we are demanding more from them and they are responding.'*

The NNP conduct their own tests of pupils' levels of achievement, and the Numeracy consultant evaluates the project each term. Class teachers evaluate pupil progress through assessments twice a term, and through group target setting, which is reviewed termly. Individual children set their own targets in mathematics, English and science, which are reviewed each term by teachers and children.

The school has found that the children have made 'marked improvements' on the NNP tests. The school has also tracked the mathematics attainment of the children who took the Key Stage 1 assessments in 1996 (the year before the strategy was introduced) by using the optional Year 4 assessments in 1998. The results showed that this group had increased their attainment levels. In 1996, 36 per cent of the children achieved Level 2 (eight per cent 2a, 16 per cent 2b and 12 per cent 2c) and 20 per cent achieved Level 3. By 1998, the children had made good progress: 40 per cent achieved Level 3 and a further 40 per cent achieved Level 4.

Although convinced of its benefits, staff recognised that implementing the Project required a lot of preparation in terms of releasing teachers to

What makes it work?

The staff felt that the NNP worked effectively for two main reasons. First, because the framework provides teachers with a focus on specific learning areas together with achievable targets. Second, setting by ability has allowed teachers to work more efficiently. Other important factors in the success of the Project included the support from the numeracy consultant and the fact that staff were committed, enthusiastic, able to communicate effectively and worked well as a team. One class teacher said: *'We've got all staff saying "Yes, this is going to work"... they wanted to do it, it's been exciting, it's been enjoyable.'*

One year after the implementation of the NNP, the only change that teachers could identify was that their curriculum planning had become much tighter. In terms of setting, the school initially attempted to set by ability across the whole of KS2 but has moved to setting by ability within the top two and bottom two junior years. This was because older children assigned to lower-ability sets found it disheartening to be grouped with children up to three years younger than themselves, and teachers found it difficult to find a teaching approach that was suitable for such a wide age-range.

take part in training, monitoring, acquiring resource materials and converting the Numeracy Framework into lesson plans. They felt that it would be some time before the Framework became fully embedded within the culture of the school. A number of teachers also pointed out that difficulties arose when new members of staff arrived at the school who had not been trained to deliver the NNP.

Teachers suggested that while the NNP appeared to be effective for the majority of children, a small number of individual pupils with statements of special educational needs did not seem to be benefiting as much. The head explained that the NNP recommends that teachers should teach to the middle ability range.

The wider the ability range within the class, the more difficult it is to engage all the children. Children with learning difficulties sometimes find the work too difficult, or struggle to keep up with the pace. The head suggested that, ideally, an additional member of staff could help support such children within the class, or children could be withdrawn from mathematics lessons. However, both of these solutions would require additional funding.

In future, teachers would like to see the Numeracy Strategy develop more support materials and would welcome more suggestions for games and activities to use in class. They would also like more attention to be paid to supporting parents in helping their children with mathematics.

Main advantages of this strategy

For pupils

- The increased pace of lessons and the use of challenging, enjoyable tasks, means that pupils find lessons more stimulating and enjoyable.

- The emphasis on active participation ensures that all pupils are involved and are encouraged to share their reasoning collectively.

- The children become more able to understand and talk about mathematical concepts.

- Children improve their ability to calculate mentally.

For teachers

- The NNP focuses teaching on specific learning areas and provides clear targets.

- The increased pace of lessons leads to a more lively delivery and a greater degree of teacher – pupil interaction.

- The increased use of team work and training opportunities have improved teachers' confidence in teaching mathematics

- Teachers are more actively involved in teaching mathematics. This has contributed to greater job satisfaction.

For the school

- Participation in the NNP has led to an increased enthusiasm for mathematics throughout the school, and has improved teamwork, planning and teaching delivery.

- The NNP provided funding, training, materials and support.

- The Project has enabled the school to tackle an area of weakness while instilling confidence in teachers.

For parents

- Parents are pleased with their children's greater progress in mathematics and now have higher expectations of their children's mathematics ability.

Main disadvantages

- The wider the range of ability within the class, the more difficult it is to pitch the teaching at the appropriate level. The small number of children with special educational needs did not appear to benefit to the same extent as other children.

- The strategy required considerable expenditure on training and materials.

- New staff joining the school need training in using the NNP.

References

HARLEN, W. and MALCOLM, H. (1997). *Setting and Streaming: a Review of Research* (Using Research Series 18). Edinburgh: SCRE.

NUMERACY TASK FORCE (1998). *The Implementation of the National Numeracy Strategy: the Final Report of the Numeracy Task Force.* London: DfEE.

OFFICE FOR STANDARDS IN EDUCATION (1998a). *Setting in Primary Schools.* London: OFSTED.

REYNOLDS, D. and MUIJS, D. (1999). *National Numeracy Strategy: an Annotated Bibliography for Teachers and Schools.* London: DfEE, Standards and Effectiveness Unit.

SUKHNANDAN, L. with LEE, B. (1998). *Streaming, Setting and Grouping by Ability: a Review of the Literature.* Slough: NFER.

Further reading on mathematics

NATIONAL NUMERACY PROJECT (1998). *Numeracy Lessons*. London: BEAM.

FIELKER, D. (1993). *Starting from Your Head: Mental Geometry*. London: BEAM.

FIELKER, D. (1993). *Starting from Your Head: Mental Number*. London: BEAM.

Further reading on setting

HARLEN, W. and MALCOLM, H. (1997). *Setting and Streaming: a Review of Research* (Using Research Series 18). Edinburgh: SCRE.

OFFICE FOR STANDARDS IN EDUCATION (1998a). *Setting in Primary Schools*. London: OFSTED.

SUKHNANDAN, L. with LEE, B. (1998). *Streaming, Setting and Grouping by Ability: a Review of the Literature*. Slough: NFER.

Addressing Underachievement of Ethnic Minority Children in Mathematics

Ferndale Primary School has a high proportion of children from Pakistani backgrounds, many of whom do not speak English at home. The school has introduced a range of strategies aimed at raising achievement in mathematics. The strategies include: recruiting additional staff and releasing teachers to work together; developing an intensive intervention programme for mathematics focusing on pupils' language needs; reorganising the school timetable; setting pupils by ability; and participating in the National Numeracy Project.

Introduction

There has been growing concern about English pupils' level of achievement in mathematics in relation to that of children in other countries (Harris *et al.*, 1997). In response, experts in the field have put forward a wide range of suggestions to address this issue, many of which have been incorporated into the National Numeracy Strategy (Numeracy Task Force, 1998; Reynolds and Muijs, 1999). There is also evidence that children from Pakistani backgrounds are underachieving at school (Gillborn and Gipps, 1996; OFSTED, 1999b).

About the school

Ferndale is an inner-city primary school in an area of social deprivation and high unemployment. It serves a community of mainly Asian heritage and the majority of its pupils are of Pakistani descent. There are about 400 children on roll, and over 90 per cent speak English as an additional language. The school has two classes in each year from reception to Year 4, and three mixed Year 5/6 classes, making a total of 13 classes.

The development of the strategies

In 1995, about two years after the appointment of a new headteacher, Ferndale was inspected by OFSTED. The inspectors' report concluded that standards in mathematics were below average, and it highlighted teachers' levels of expertise and low expectations as areas of concern. In order to address these issues, the head decided to implement a number of strategies aimed at supporting staff and raising pupils' achievement, particularly in mathematics.

When the headteacher joined the school, she devoted a period of time to sorting out the school's budget and discovered that there was room for making savings. The head and governors made the decision to prioritise the recruitment of additional staff, so part of the school budget was specifically set aside for this purpose. Careful consideration was given to the level of staff that were recruited. For example, when experienced (and relatively expensive) members of staff left the school, they were replaced with less experienced, less expensive staff. At the time of the 1996 inspection, the school employed 16 full-time equivalent teachers. By 1998, there were 22 teachers on the staff, 20 of whom worked at the school full-time.

When a new mathematics coordinator joined the school, the head suggested that she should apply for funding under the LEA's school improvement project. This provided the funds and support to research and implement new strategies and to spread good practice throughout the school. Once accepted on to the project, the LEA allocated a grant of £4,000, which the school matched from its own budget. The scheme provided a structure for school improvement: the school set up a small steering group of four teachers and a larger project team (involving teachers, support staff, governors, parents

and pupils). An LEA adviser helped them to evaluate the initiative by setting up a database for recording children's test scores and advising on evaluation questionnaires.

The following year, the head nominated the school to take part in the pilot of the National Numeracy Project (NNP) because she felt it represented a natural progression of their own initiative. The NNP provided the school with a small amount of funding which the school again had to match from its own budget. The funding received from both the LEA and NNP was used primarily for supply cover to release the mathematics coordinator and to purchase new resources, such as calculators. Prior to the introduction of the NNP, two members of staff attended an NNP training week and disseminated the information to the rest of the staff. In addition, an NNP consultant visited the school to provide training for all staff.

The strategies

One of the first changes introduced by the head was to reorganise the school timetable. She lengthened the morning session in order to provide three full hours of teaching time. Secondly, she decided to deploy the additional staff to enable staff to work together. Teachers are released in pairs for two hours of non-contact time per week. They use this time to support one another's development, discuss

the children's progress, and plan further work for their classes. The introduction of this 'simultaneous release time' was aimed at raising teachers' expectations and improving staff expertise.

In response to the problem of underachievement, staff decided to introduce setting by ability for mathematics. They believed that

because setting would reduce the range of ability within a class, teachers would be better able to meet the needs of all the children. Assessment results are used to set pupils across two year-groups (Years 5 and 6, and Years 3 and 4) into three ability bands. The extra members of staff are used to split the KS2 classes into 14 groups, thereby halving the size of the teaching groups. Setting is applied flexibly so that pupils can be moved into different groups at any time.

The mathematics coordinator decided to focus on the needs of children in Years 3 and 4 whose mathematics attainment was 'just below average'. These pupils were identified by administering a standardised mathematics test to all pupils in the two year-groups.

(The school decided to use standardised tests because these provide a reliable score in relation to a child's age.)

Fourteen pupils from each year-group were chosen to participate in the programme. In order to clarify the nature of pupils' difficulties with mathematics, the mathematics coordinator interviewed all the selected pupils and compiled a report for the steering group. The interviews revealed that children had a limited concept of mathematics and did not see its relevance outside school. The coordinator noticed that the children were restricted in their use of mathematical vocabulary and realised that this hindered their ability to discuss their work or to identify what they had learned. On the positive side, most of the children said they enjoyed maths and had people at home who could help with their maths homework. A bilingual teacher added to the information-gathering by conducting interviews with the children's parents.

In response to the coordinator's report, the steering group decided to concentrate on improving children's mathematical vocabulary. The content of the programme was based on schemes of work that were already in place at the school. The coordinator designed a new lesson structure, which consisted of a ten-minute introduction based on learning relevant mathematical vocabulary, followed by 30 minutes in which pupils worked in pairs on an activity designed to generate discussion. The lessons ended with a ten-minute plenary in which children were asked to explain to the rest of the class what they had been doing. At the end of each lesson, children were given mathematical activities which their parents helped them to complete at home.

The targeted pupils were withdrawn from their regular mathematics lessons for an hour a day for four weeks. The head taught the Year 3 pupils and the coordinator taught the Year 4 pupils. At the end of the course, the school celebrated the children's achievements by awarding prizes and certificates to the children and their parents.

Following the success of this initiative, a number of teachers decided to adopt similar teaching methods with their own classes. When the school began taking part in the NNP, there were many similarities. One class teacher said: *'The Numeracy Project came in at Easter but by the time that came in we had already had our project up and running ... there were a lot of comparisons, so really the Numeracy Project just sort of took over from our schemes of work and our planning.'*

Are the strategies successful?

The staff committed themselves to setting up a monitoring and evaluation system as part of their project. The teachers and parents on the school improvement team observed some of the lessons. The LEA adviser helped the teachers to evaluate the project's impact by using standardised mathematics tests administered before and after the introduction of the initiative. The mathematics coordinator carried out interviews with teachers and pupils and sent questionnaires to parents.

The quality of lessons now is better, expertise of staff has gone up massively, the planning is far more to the point and pertinent.

Responses to the initiative were very positive. The mathematics test scores for children taking part the in programme increased by an average of nine points, whereas the scores of children who did not participate did not increase. Retests six months later showed that the targeted pupils had maintained their improved attainment. As a result of their involvement in this project, the school won a National Primary Centre Award for school improvement.

Staff welcomed the subsequent introduction of the NNP. They felt it allowed them to teach mathematics far more efficiently and effectively. One KS2 class teacher reflected: *'Overall, you think that you're teaching maths quite successfully but when you look through the Numeracy Project, the guidelines for mental activities, and all the language and the open-ended questions, you actually realise that before, you were stunting how the children could progress.'*

Another teacher commented on the way that the NNP had increased children's enthusiasm for mathematics: *'At the end of the day they will ask for maths games before they go home, in the last few minutes. It's nice to see them buzzing and full of enthusiasm.'*

The head felt that as a result of all their initiatives, the children were receiving an enhanced learning experience. She felt that planning and delivery have improved because staff work more collaboratively: *'The quality of lessons now is better, expertise of staff has gone up massively, the planning is far more to the point and pertinent. So what the children are getting is considerably better.'*

The NNP is currently being monitored and evaluated through classroom observations and NNP tests. Although initial results look promising, they have yet to be finalised. Because they introduced several new initiatives simultaneously, staff pointed out that it is not possible to attribute increases in children's attainment to any one strategy.

The school received a strong endorsement of its efforts as the result of an HMI inspection in the summer of 1997. The purpose of the visit was to assess the school's progress in tackling the areas of weakness identified during the previous inspection. The report reached a positive conclusion, stating: *'The headteacher has been successful in taking the school forward. Many initiatives have been undertaken for school improvement and a number of these are having a positive impact on standards.'* In relation to mathematics, the report said: *'Pupils make sound progress in all aspects of mathematics. The school has made considerable efforts to improve numeracy and is successfully raising standards.'* The inspection team concluded that such good progress had been made that there was no further need for OFSTED to monitor its action plan.

What makes it work?

This school faces the challenge teaching children from socially deprived backgrounds for whom English is a second language. The OFSTED inspection pointed out specific weaknesses in staff expertise and expectations, and identified a problem of underachievement. In response, the headteacher and governors implemented a number of strategies to support staff and to improve children's attainment.

The head appointed a new mathematics coordinator, who interviewed the children in order to clarify the reasons for underachievement. When it became apparent that children needed support with their mathematical vocabulary, the school responded by introducing an intensive programme to address the problem. The LEA's school improvement project

provided funding, advice and a sound structure for the management and evaluation of the project's impact.

Staff felt that the main reasons for the success of the strategies were the high expectations of project leaders and the enthusiasm and commitment of staff to school improvement. The head suggested that in order for the strategies to work effectively they had to be targeted accurately in terms of year groups and pupils. In terms of staffing, she suggested that the different projects should be led by people who had the skills to ensure that the strategies were successfully implemented. The senior management team needed to understand the responsibilities and pressures on staff and to provide them with support. There was also a need to underpin all initiatives with adequate systems (such as timetabling and decisions about the use of resources) to facilitate success and ensure that the school was getting the best value for money.

Although the teachers were very positive about the results of their school improvement strategies, they recognised that there had been some difficulties and disadvantages. For example,

although the reorganisation of the school timetable had brought about additional learning time, one of the teachers pointed out that this had reduced children's opportunities to let off steam, relax and socialise during playtime.

In terms of the limitations of the NNP, some staff felt that its detailed planning placed limits on the ability of teachers to use their own professional judgement. Teachers also pointed out that difficulties arose when new members of staff joined the school who had no previous training in how to implement the NNP.

Interestingly, although the children we spoke to were in favour of their new mathematics lessons, a couple of the Year 5 and 6 pupils felt that whole-class teaching was holding them back (even though they were taught in ability groups). One said: *'We're old enough to know what we have to do; all we have to do is read the book and we'll get on with it and we'll do more maths.'* Another said: *'It's a bit boring sometimes, 'cos some people don't understand so you have to go over it again and you just have to sit there.'*

The teachers felt that their own school improvement programme was particularly helpful for raising children's attainment, so they are planning to rerun it in future. However, they intend to modify the programme by using it with mixed-ability groups and by reducing the programme from four weeks to two weeks to enable a greater number of children to participate.

Main advantages of this strategy

For pupils

- Children are making better progress in mathematics.

- Their enjoyment of mathematics has increased.

- Pupils were represented on the school improvement steering group.

- The strategies have improved pupils' ability to discuss mathematical concepts. They have opportunities to develop their vocabulary and oral language skills.

For teachers

- The strategies have had a positive impact on teachers' confidence in teaching mathematics, and the quality of their instruction has improved.

- Teachers have opportunities to plan together and to work collaboratively within school time.

- Setting by ability and dividing the year-groups into smaller teaching units make it easier to target teaching at the right level.

- The use of games and whole-class interactive teaching generates children's enthusiasm for mathematics.

For parents

- Parents were represented on the school improvement steering group.

- Parents are better informed about their child's attainment and are more involved in helping their child to make progress at school.

For the school

- The strategies have helped to emphasise the importance of mathematics throughout the school.

- The school's mathematics results have improved.

- Governors, parents, pupils and teachers worked together to improve the school's performance. There is an increased level of enthusiasm among staff and a strong commitment to school improvement.

- The school's successes have been recognised through a positive HMI report and a national award for school improvement.

Main disadvantages

- Although reorganising the timetable provided more time for learning, this has been achieved by reducing children's time for play.

- Teachers feel that their room for exercising professional judgement is curtailed to some extent by the detailed lesson plans set out in the NNP.

- Some children can feel frustrated when the teacher has to repeat work to ensure that the whole class understands.

- New staff joining the school require training in using the NNP.

References

GILLBORN, D. and GIPPS, C. (1996). *Recent Research on the Achievements of Ethnic Minority Pupils* (OFSTED Reviews of Research). London: HMSO.

HARRIS, S., KEYS, W. and FERNANDES, C. (1997). *Third International Mathematics and Science Study, Second National Report. Part 1: Achievement in Mathematics and Science at Age 9 in England.* Slough: NFER.

NUMERACY TASK FORCE (1998). *The Implementation of the National Numeracy Strategy: the Final Report of the Numeracy Task Force.* London: DfEE.

OFSTED (1999b). *Raising the Attainment of Minority Ethnic Pupils: School and LEA Responses.* London: OFSTED.

REYNOLDS, D. and MUIJS, D. (1999). *National Numeracy Strategy: an Annotated Bibliography for Teachers and Schools.* London: DfEE, Standards and Effectiveness Unit.

Further reading on mathematics

NATIONAL NUMERACY PROJECT (1998). *Numeracy Lessons*. London: BEAM.

FIELKER, D. (1993). *Starting from Your Head: Mental Geometry*. London: BEAM.

FIELKER, D. (1993). *Starting from Your Head: Mental Number*. London: BEAM.

SCHOOL CURRICULUM AND ASSESSMENT AUTHORITY (1997). *Mathematics and the Use of Language: Key Stages 1 & 2*. London: SCAA.

Further reading on setting

HARLEN, W. and MALCOLM, H. (1997). *Setting and Streaming: a Review of Research* (Using Research Series 18). Edinburgh: SCRE.

OFFICE FOR STANDARDS IN EDUCATION (1998). *Setting in Primary Schools*. London: OFSTED.

SUKHNANDAN, L. with LEE, B. (1998). *Streaming, Setting and Grouping by Ability: a Review of the Literature*. Slough: NFER.

Further reading on the needs of children from ethnic minorities

GILLBORN, D. and GIPPS, C. (1996). *Recent Research on the Achievements of Ethnic Minority Pupils* (OFSTED Reviews of Research). London: HMSO.

OFFICE FOR STANDARDS IN EDUCATION (1999). *Raising the Attainment of Minority Ethnic Pupils: School and LEA Responses*. London: OFSTED.

Subject Specialist Teaching

Tamhurst Primary School has introduced subject specialist teaching for all children in Key Stage 2. Teachers specialise in one of four foundation subjects (music, design and technology, history and geography).

Introduction

One of the big challenges facing all schools at Key Stage 2 is how to cover the whole curriculum in sufficient depth. Traditionally, children in each class have received almost all of their teaching from one teacher. This has undoubted benefits in terms of the emotional security of the children, the social cohesion of the class and the ability of the teacher to plan a coherent set of experiences for the children. However, the traditional model is coming under increased scrutiny: to what extent can the benefits of the class teacher model be reconciled with the demands of curriculum coverage at KS2?

About the school

Tamhurst Primary is based in a small town in a rural area. The 223 children come from predominantly white families based in the town and the surrounding villages and hamlets. Ten per cent of the children are eligible for free school meals, and nine per cent are identified as having special educational needs. In the 1960s, the school relocated to its current premises, which were originally occupied by a secondary school. The school has one class per year group (i.e.

seven classes, from reception to Year 6) and there is a playgroup on site.

Development of the strategy

Subject specialist teaching was first introduced into the school in the late 1980s, when the school had fewer children on roll. The school needed to provide more challenging work in history and geography, because this was identified as a weakness as a result of an HMI inspection. The senior management team decided to reassess their use of a 'topic-based' teaching approach. They applied to an LEA curriculum development scheme for funding to enable a support teacher to work in the school.

As a result of their successful grant application, a teacher was employed to teach history to the juniors on four afternoons a week. This enabled three mixed-age classes to be split into four year

groups in the afternoons, and helped the school to address the needs of the junior children who were in mixed-age classes. In 1992, following an internal review which confirmed the success of the initiative, it was decided to implement subject teaching more widely at KS2, using existing staff.

The strategy

The four KS2 classes have subject specialist teaching four times a week. The specialist subjects are: music, design and technology, history and geography. Each year-group have their own class teacher for lessons in mathematics, English, science, art, RE and PE.

On four afternoons each week, children move to one of the four Key Stage 2 classes for a subject-based lesson (teachers remain in their own classrooms, which serve as a resource base for their subject teaching). The lessons last for a period of one-and-a-half hours,

before the children return to their own classrooms for the final 45 minutes of the school day. On Friday afternoons, all four classes have art activities, which are taught by their own class teachers.

Specialist teachers are responsible for planning and teaching their subject area across KS2. They also act as subject coordinators throughout the school, overseeing lesson plans and giving advice and guidance for teachers in the infant classes. The specialist teachers provide information to parents on the work their child will be covering in the subject during the coming term. They are also responsible for reporting on the progress of all the KS2 children in their subject area.

Is it successful?

The teachers believed that they had achieved a good balance between class teaching and subject specialism. As one teacher commented: *'We've got the best of both worlds.'* They did not want to lose the class teaching element and would not have wished to be subject teachers all the time. They pointed out that they were able to develop a close working relationship with their own class, to whom they teach six subjects (i.e. the three core subjects plus PE, RE and their specialist subject). On the other hand, subject specialism gave them the satisfaction of developing expertise and managing one area of the curriculum. They preferred to use subject specialism for foundation subjects, because they felt it was important for all teachers to maintain their involvement in teaching the core subjects to their own class.

The Year 3 and Year 6 children we spoke to said they liked the system. They welcomed the chance to get to know different members of staff, and felt this smoothed the transition from one year-group to the next. As one Year 3 child said: *'I think it's good to swap around so that when you move up a class you think: "I'm not afraid and I'm not shy with this person, 'cos I know her very well".'* The children recognised that their subject teachers had specialist knowledge: *'You can learn different things from different teachers, 'cos one teacher might know more than another.'* They felt that subject teaching made school more interesting, and that it would help to prepare them for subject specialist teaching at secondary school.

I think it's good to swap around so that when you move up a class you think: "I'm not afraid and I'm not shy with this person, 'cos I know her very well".

The school has attempted to evaluate and monitor the impact of subject specialism through surveys and staff discussion. Shortly after it was first introduced, teachers evaluated the impact of specialist teaching, by sending

questionnaires to governors, parents and pupils. The results revealed that the majority of parents and governors were aware of the changes that had been made and considered them to have had a positive impact. Pupils said they enjoyed having different teachers, but they also noted one initial drawback: namely a loss of time for art activities. This issue was addressed by ensuring that a period on Friday afternoons was set aside for art.

The headteacher believed that there was evidence of a steady improvement in all curriculum areas including in the pace of teaching and learning, and the quality of planning, communication and tracking of pupil progress. Subject leaders were beginning to set targets for their areas. For example the subject leader for design and technology set a target for 80 per cent of Year 6 children to reach Level 4 in 1998 (an increase of four per cent over the previous year). In the event, the children met this target, with 17 per cent of them achieving Level 5.

A 1996 OFSTED inspection report commended the school's approach, saying: *'This school has introduced an imaginative, effective and well coordinated approach to specialist teaching of the foundation subjects of the National Curriculum at Key Stage 2. It has achieved a level of self-evaluation which is excellent and thus informs the strategic direction of the school.'*

The staff could identify few drawbacks to their initiative, but they did acknowledge that there is a certain lack of flexibility in the system. For example, if children are unable to complete a task, subject teachers cannot easily arrange for an extra session to help them catch up.

Subject specialism also makes an additional call on teachers' time. The school no longer receives additional funding for the initiative, and there is little non-contact time available (in fact, teachers have only one morning per term for subject planning). Report writing is time-consuming because, in addition to reporting on their own class, each teacher has to comment on the progress of all KS2 pupils in their subject area (although this is balanced by the fact that they do not have to report on children's progress in three subjects).

However, staff felt that these were minor drawbacks to a successful initiative. They suggested that a similar approach could work well in other schools, provided that the staff are enthusiastic about the initiative and the implementation takes account of the size and organisation of the school.

What makes it work?

This school chose to adopt a limited form of subject specialism in response to a weakness in subject teaching identified by HMI. When the initiative proved successful, staff decided to adopt subject specialism more widely at KS2. They monitored and evaluated the early stages of their initiative and have adapted it to address the needs of pupils and staff. The initiative is underpinned with a system of thorough planning and discussion

and there are opportunities for staff development.

The subject coordinators have embarked on a process of auditing each subject area. Each term, two areas are reviewed. The review focuses on standards achieved, teaching strengths and weaknesses, resources and areas for development. This structured examination of each subject helps to identify any areas in need of materials, teaching and learning resources or training. The results of the audits are discussed among the teaching staff and the Governors' Curriculum Committee. The audit forms the basis for decisions to allocate resources to each area.

Communication between teachers is a key element. The school has an annual curriculum planning day, during which teachers map all the experiences that children will encounter in the year. This gives them an opportunity to share information and to plan links across subjects, where appropriate.

Staff have opportunities to update their knowledge through training: the school applies for places on INSET courses, according to the needs and priorities identified in the school development plan. For example, when a new teacher without experience of specialist teaching joined the staff, she took part in a ten-day course to help develop her knowledge in geography.

Since the initiative started, the teachers have decided to change their approach to

curriculum planning. Rather than teaching up to four different units at once, they found it works better to teach the same unit to all four year-groups simultaneously (while pitching at the appropriate level for each class). This means that planning is more focused and resources are used more efficiently. It also enables staff to arrange activities involving the whole of the juniors (for example, several classes worked together to decorate a corridor as a rain forest for a recent geography project, and the whole school joined together to re-enact a 'Victorian Day').

Postscript

Since our visit, the school has introduced subject specialist teaching for PE. Time spent on subject teaching has been reduced by half an hour to a one-hour period for each subject, in response to the introduction of the Literacy and Numeracy Hours.

Main advantages of this strategy

For pupils

- Subject specialism enables children to get to know all the KS2 staff, which makes the change of class teacher each year less daunting.

- Children benefit from being taught by someone who knows their subject well and is enthusiastic about their own area of the curriculum.

- Teachers can ensure that children have a continuity of experience throughout KS2.

- Being taught by different teachers in the afternoon helps to maintain children's interest and levels of concentration.

- Children gain an understanding of subject identity: they have a sense of the important characteristics of each subject.

- Teachers can identify children with aptitude in a specific subject and can nurture individual talent and interest.

- Children feel better prepared for subject teaching in the secondary school.

For teachers

- Teachers do not have to attempt to cover all subjects: everyone has a clear understanding of what they do (and do not) need to teach to their own class.

- Teachers can develop specific subject expertise: they have major responsibility for planning and delivering 'their' subject to all the junior children.

- Teachers have the opportunity to get to know all of the junior pupils well.

- Teachers get the satisfaction of seeing children progress in one subject over a period of four years.

- Subject specialist teaching provides enhanced opportunities for job satisfaction, access to training and career development.

For the school

- Curriculum planning and needs identification have become more effective. Subject auditing contributes to a process of whole-school development.

- The school has been commended by OFSTED for its approach to curriculum coverage.

- The school is able to target professional development where it is likely to have an impact on the greatest number of children.

For parents

- Teachers provide parents with an outline of what their child will be covering in each area of the curriculum during the forthcoming term.

- Parents receive well-informed reports on their child's progress in each subject area and can speak to a specialist teacher if they have any concerns about their child's progress.

Main disadvantages

- Teachers miss out on teaching three areas of the curriculum. It is possible that this could cause problems for teachers wishing to move to other schools.

- There is a certain loss in flexibility: teachers cannot easily arrange for extra time to enable children to catch up with their subject work.

- There is an additional workload on teachers, who are responsible for planning, delivering and reporting on children's progress in one subject for all Key Stage 2 classes (although this is balanced by not having to teach three subject areas).

Further reading on subject specialist teaching

OFFICE FOR STANDARDS IN EDUCATION (1997). *Using Subject Specialists to Promote High Standards at Key Stage 2: an Illustrative Survey.* London: OFSTED.

Challenging Higher-Attaining Children

Seaview Primary School has introduced a number of strategies to challenge higher-attaining children in their English, mathematics and science. These include changes to the pace and content of lessons, more open-ended tasks and more frequent use of interactive whole-class teaching.

Introduction

The Government has set ambitious targets for the performance of children in National Curriculum assessments at KS2. However, there is a potential danger that schools will concentrate on children at the Level 3/4 borderline, with less attention given to low achievers or to pupils who are already capable of achieving Level 4. After addressing the needs of lower attainers, Seaview Primary School has turned its attention to stretching the higher-achieving children in the school.

About the school

Seaview Primary School is a voluntary-controlled church school. The school serves two neighbouring villages and has 82 children on its roll, from reception to Year 6. There are two KS2 classes in the school: a mixed Year 3 and 4 class and a mixed Year 5 and 6 class. Children come from a range of backgrounds. Some are drawn from professional families who have moved to the area, others from families who have lived in the villages for many generations. Although there is some rural deprivation in the area, only ten children are entitled to free school meals. There are nine children on the special needs register.

The development of the strategy

Following the arrival of a new headteacher in 1995, the school introduced standardised assessments in reading and mathematics to monitor the progress of the children and the value added by the school. The head began a period of team building and policy development, involving all staff. As part of their commitment to school improvement, staff reviewed their coverage of the curriculum. Addressing the needs of lower-attaining children was identified as an early priority, and measures were introduced to ensure that these children were supported.

An OFSTED inspection in 1996 confirmed that the school was performing well in relation to national standards, but identified the need to extend the higher-attaining children. In its key issues for action, the OFSTED report stated: *'To further improve the standards of education and quality of learning, the governors, headteacher and staff should take steps to challenge more rigorously the most able pupils through extension and enrichment activities.'*

After the inspection, the head decided to research the needs of higher-attaining children for an MA module in strategic management. She attended two conferences on teaching the more able child, and read a number of books on the subject.

In the autumn of 1996, the head sent a questionnaire to all teachers, parents and governors. This asked if they felt that the needs of higher-attaining children were being met by the school and what, if anything, could be done to challenge these children further. Everyone was in agreement that although the school was already doing well, there was room for improvement for higher attainers. In addition, the head spoke to a small number of children who had achieved high test scores to determine the extent to which they felt they were being challenged at school. Children said they learned most when they enjoyed their lessons and found it helpful when teachers taught by using examples. They found worksheets boring, but enjoyed conducting their own research and going on visits which were later followed up in class.

After the responses from the questionnaires and interviews had been analysed, the staff met to discuss how they could best support this group of children. The next step was to identify the children who would be expected to benefit from the new strategies. They decided to focus on children with 'above-average' scores in relation to national norms (those who scored 110 or more in standardised non-verbal reasoning tests). Specific target scores were set for this group of children to achieve in their National Curriculum assessments, and in standardised tests of reading and mathematics.

In 1997, the school set aside £150 from the school budget for the work on challenging higher-attaining children. Staff used the money to buy new resources for English, mathematics and science, to enable teachers to undertake more investigative work and to stretch the higher-attaining children by offering more challenging reading books. The school subscribed to the National Association for Able Children in Education. In addition, money

from GEST and the Standards Fund was used to pay for travel, fees and supply cover to enable teachers to attend relevant conferences, meetings and training sessions.

The strategy

On the basis of the head's research and their own experience, the staff decided to use a number of different methods to challenge higher-attaining children in the school. These included paying attention to the pace, content and organisation of lessons and providing opportunities for higher attainers to demonstrate and share their skills. The teachers identified 14 children as higher attainers on the basis of the standardised non-verbal reasoning test results. Rather than devise teaching approaches aimed exclusively at these children (such as one-to-one teaching or ability grouping), it was decided to focus on strategies that would benefit the whole class.

The teachers decided to reduce the amount of time they asked children to work through exercises in textbooks and to introduce more open-ended, problem-solving tasks.

The teachers decided to place particular emphasis on challenging children in reading and mathematics because they felt that achievement in these two areas had a substantial impact on the school curriculum as a whole. The content of lessons was changed to include more challenging concepts. For example, the head commented: *'In maths we're doing lots more work on fractions with the seven- and eight-year-olds than we have ever done before. I've never taught seven-year-olds alliteration before but this year I thought: "Well, why not?".'*

In the 1997–98 academic year, the staff began to explore the benefits for higher-attaining children of interactive whole-class teaching. After watching a video on this teaching method (OFSTED, 1997) and discussing its possible application, all teachers agreed to introduce more whole-class teaching into their lessons.

Teachers felt that giving children more opportunities to share their work with others in their class would motivate the higher attainers. They decided to celebrate the achievements of higher-attaining children, as well

During our visit to the school, we observed a Year 5/6 science lesson, in which the teacher had planned to keep children motivated by involving them in a practical investigation and keeping up the pace of activities. The children were required to separate a mixture of sand, salt, iron filings and water using the processes of filtration, magnetism, evaporation and condensation. The class teacher ensured that the lesson moved at a rapid pace by giving the children short blocks of time to carry out experiments and to complete written work. These were interspersed with whole-class work during which the teacher followed up the work with rapid-fire question-and-answer sessions.

The children kept up a high level of concentration throughout the lesson. They appeared to find the experimental work interesting and enjoyable. The questions asked by the teachers were challenging, but children were keen to contribute and to discuss the results of their experiments.

We observed an English lesson for children in Years 3 and 4. The class had recently visited a local farm, and the teacher drew on this experience as a stimulus for poetry writing. The lesson began with a question-and-answer session about the farm visit, in which the teacher focused on the detail of their experiences and the language used on the farm. In addition to writing poems, the children were encouraged to use the correct terms for different types of imagery. Almost all the children in the class were able to use terms such as 'alliteration', 'simile', 'rhyming couplet' and 'onomatopoeia' correctly and with confidence. The teacher commented that, before the able child strategy was introduced, she would not have attempted to introduce this material to children in Years 3 and 4.

as praising the efforts of the less able. Local and national competitions were used to motivate the higher-attaining children, in the belief that able children work best if they have a definite goal for their work.

I've never taught seven-year-olds alliteration before but this year I thought: "Well, why not?".

The school has also expanded the extracurricular activities available to children. These include sports teams, music tuition and bird watching. Teachers have strengthened their links with the local community, and children make visits to the church and to local businesses. Each year, children in Year 6 travel to France with children from neighbouring primary schools who will be transferring to the same secondary school.

Is it successful?

Since the introduction of the 'able child' project, teachers have become much more aware of the issue and have increased their expectations of what children can achieve. Tasks have become more challenging and the pace of lessons has increased. Staff are convinced that the higher-attaining children have been increasingly challenged since they began their initiatives in this area. The Year 5/6 teacher was enthusiastic about the benefits of interactive whole-class teaching: *'The whole class teaching doesn't allow them to switch off. You keep bringing them back into it with questions until they realise they have to join in. You get to know what they understand and what they don't.'*

Children were also able to identify benefits from their experiences. They particularly enjoyed taking part in the visits and extracurricular activities, saying that such experiences helped them to work as a team and to get on with other people.

The LEA has taken note of the success of this work, and has invited the school to contribute to a publication on higher-attaining children, to be shared with other schools.

The results of the standardised tests have shown some improvement over the last academic year, with most children showing gains, particularly in mathematics. The Year 5/6 teacher commented on the mathematics results for Year 6: *'The average standardised score went up from 99 to about 107! Eight points! This could just be a one-off, but the change seems quite staggering. It's a bit worrying because it indicates that for the last couple of years we have been underachieving.'*

The school has decided to use the KS2 results as success criteria for the strategy. They set an ambitious target for a quarter of

the children to reach Level 5 in English, mathematics and science at KS2. The 1998 results showed that 20 per cent of children had attained Level 5 in English and ten per cent in science. None of the group achieved Level 5 in mathematics, although some of them missed it by two or three marks (the head pointed out that the introduction of a new mental arithmetic assessment in 1988 had depressed children's mathematics scores).

This could just be a one-off, but the change seems quite staggering.

Teachers identified few disadvantages to the able child initiative. However, they acknowledged that whole-class teaching had not benefited a child with identified moderate learning difficulties. There was also some concern that lower-attaining children could be disadvantaged by adopting whole-class teaching, because they may miss out on specific attention devoted to their needs. However, the head felt that this could be overcome with differentiated question-and-answer sessions. Another possible drawback is the additional amount of time that staff have committed to planning for English, mathematics and science, which are the focus for the able children work. The head acknowledged that staff did not have as much time as usual

to plan for other subjects, particularly arts and crafts activities.

What makes it work?

Extending the higher-attaining children was highlighted as a priority in the school's OFSTED inspection. The headteacher researched the issue thoroughly, involving governors, parents, staff and pupils in the process of clarifying the needs of higher-attaining children and identifying strategies to meet their needs. The plans for action were clearly stated and agreed by all staff. The head monitored the implementation of the strategies through discussion and classroom observation.

The strategy has been characterised by clear target setting. The higher-attaining children were identified using agreed criteria, and targets were set for improvements in achievement. Children were involved in individual target setting too, and anyone who made gains in relation to their previous test scores was praised for their achievement.

The head believed that the teaching methods were central to the success of the strategy. Pitching lessons at a higher level and challenging the children to a greater extent were the key factors. This has led to increased expectations of the higher-attaining children by both teachers and parents.

The average standardised score went up from 99 to about 107!

The strategies have become embedded in the practice of the school. The importance of this area has been recognised through the establishment of a post of responsibility for able children and a written policy has been produced, which is a useful reference point for teachers and governors.

Postscript

Since our visit, the deputy head has taken major responsibility for able pupils. In 1998, the staff encouraged a child in Year 5 to take the KS2 mathematics assessment, and he achieved Level 5. The school has since provided additional support for this child and one other to enable them to work on the mathematics curriculum for Level 6.

Main advantages of this strategy

For pupils

- The potential of higher-attaining children has been recognised and their successes are rewarded.

- Higher-attaining children are challenged during their English, mathematics and science lessons and their attainment increases.

- Lessons are more interesting for all children: they are taught at a faster pace and have more opportunities for practical work.

- Children are given increased opportunities to pursue their interests through a variety of extracurricular clubs and school visits.

- Children receive feedback on their progress and are involved in setting themselves targets for the future.

For teachers

- Teaching is more rewarding as children are challenged and their attainment levels increase.

- Whole-class interactive teaching is enjoyable for teachers. It enables the teacher to ensure that all children are paying attention and provides instant feedback on the children's grasp of the material.

For parents

- Parents have become more involved in their child's education and are better informed about their child's progress.

- Parents of higher-attaining children know that the school is addressing their child's needs.

For the school

- This project enabled the school to address a key issue for action, identified in an OFSTED inspection.

- Governors and parents were consulted and became involved in the process of school improvement.

- The school's National Curriculum assessment results have improved.

- The school has been recognised as an example of good practice within the LEA.

Main disadvantages

- More time spent on planning in mathematics, English and science has left less time for teachers to plan other areas of the curriculum.

- Whole-class teaching did not benefit a child with learning difficulties and there is some concern that lower-attaining children may not benefit to the same extent as others.

Reference

OFFICE FOR STANDARDS IN EDUCATION (1997). *Teachers Count* [Video]. London: OFSTED.

Further reading on addressing the needs of higher attaining children

EYRE, D. (1997). *Able Children in Ordinary Schools*. London: David Fulton.

FREEMAN, J. (1998). *Educating the Very Able: Current International Research* (OFSTED Reviews of Research). London: The Stationery Office.

TEARE, B. (1997). *Effective Provision for Able & Talented Children*. Stafford: Network Educational Press.

Tackling Boys' Underachievement

St George's is one of a group of schools that have become increasingly concerned about boys' underachievement. In order to address this issue, staff at St George's have adopted several strategies, all of which aim to encourage boys to contribute more positively in class. Three of the strategies adopted by the school are described below.

Introduction

The results of the National Curriculum assessments in recent years have shown that girls outperform boys at the ages of both seven and 11. According to figures published by QCA in 1998, almost three-quarters of girls achieved the expected standard in English at KS2, but only 57 per cent of boys did so (QCA, 1998b).

In order to address such gender differences, experts have suggested a range of strategies to help engage boys in the learning process, deal with poor behaviour and to raise boys' levels of achievement (see MacDonald *et al.*, 1999).

About the school

St George's is a Church of England primary school serving a village parish. The school was built to educate children from mining families, but the school's population has changed recently, due to the building of a new housing estate. About two-thirds of the 277 children come from professional families and the remaining third are from working-class, mining backgrounds. Almost all children come from white families. Eleven per cent of the pupils are eligible for free school meals, and 12 per cent are identified as having special educational needs. The school has eight mixed-age classes from reception to Year 6.

The development of the strategies

St George's is one of six primary schools forming a 'pyramid' with a local secondary school. The head of St George's explained that the impetus for their initiative came about in the mid 1990s when the head of the secondary school became concerned about boys' relatively low levels of achievement at GCSE compared with that of girls. At about the same time, the primary heads began to notice that boys were becoming *'disenchanted with education, bored and disruptive'.*

The heads of all the pyramid schools met to discuss the issue in 1996 and decided to focus on raising boys' levels of achievement. They consulted an LEA inspector who was involved in the authority's working party on equal opportunities, who encouraged them to apply for a grant from the LEA's Curriculum Project Fund. The schools used the £2,500 to buy in an independent consultant who had expertise in the area of boys' underachievement.

The six primary heads decided to pilot a range of strategies with children in Year 6. The consultant provided a one-day training session for heads and Y6 class teachers. He demonstrated a variety of techniques for involving boys more productively in the learning process. The teachers agreed to try out as many of the strategies as possible in their own classes. At the end of the pilot year, the teachers reported back on which strategies they had found most effective. Each school within the pyramid then adopted the strategies that they felt were most appropriate for them.

Following the successful implementation of the pilot stage, the consultant provided another one-day training session for all of the remaining teachers. In 1997, the strategies were implemented, in various forms, across all of the year-groups in all of the pyramid schools.

The strategies

At St George's, the KS2 staff adopted a number of strategies, three of which are described in more detail below: Circle Time, Going for Five and Mixed Gender Pairing.

Circle Time was introduced to improve listening and speaking skills and to encourage active participation from all children in the class. It was recommended to help overcome the tendency for boys to dominate class discussions, and to give all children the opportunity to express themselves in a supportive environment.

During our research at the school, we observed Circle Time in a Y5 class. It was the fist session in the morning. The children entered the classroom and sat (in boy/girl, boy/girl order) in a circle on a carpeted area. The class had recently been visited by a student teacher, who had asked the class teacher to obtain feedback from the children.

The teacher began the session by asking the children to give their comments on the student teacher's initial visit. She passed a small toy to the child sitting next to her. As the toy was passed around the circle, roughly three-quarters of the pupils contributed both positive and negative (but constructive) comments. None of the children spoke unless they had possession of the toy. Once the toy had been passed around the circle, the teacher repeated the process, asking for their suggestions about what they could do to improve the student's next visit. Children made various suggestions, including that they needed to explain more to the student teacher about some of the things they did regularly in class, such as the Going for Five technique; and that they could help him by being quieter and better behaved in class. At the end of the 15-minute session, the teacher thanked the pupils for their comments and told them that the student would be joining them for their next Circle Time later in the week.

The children sit in a circle and the teacher introduces a subject for discussion. This can range from topics related to academic work, to broader social issues. The teacher starts the discussion by passing an object (such as a beanbag or small toy) to the child sitting next to them. Children are allowed to speak only when they are holding the object. When they have finished saying what they want to, they pass the object to the next person. Anyone who doesn't wish to speak simply passes the object on.

Going for Five is a useful technique for encouraging divergent thinking and persistence. Teachers ask open-ended questions and pupils are asked to think of five or more answers. The children are given a fixed amount of time to complete the task. When the time is up, the teacher asks children for their answers. This technique is recommended for helping boys to overcome the tendency to jump to a single solution to a problem without considering alternatives.

We observed a Y6 lesson on healthy eating, in which the teacher made extensive use of the Going for Five technique. The teacher planned to cover issues of nutrition and to remind children about the basic food groups in preparation for a lesson on health and hygiene, which would be led by the school nurse.

The teacher introduced the topic by asking the children to make a note of five ways of staying healthy. The teacher told them to work in pairs and explained that they had ten minutes to complete the task. During the allocated time, the teacher circulated around the class providing advice and encouraging those who had already thought of five things to think of some more. When the time was up, the teacher asked several children to report back items from their list. She wrote their answers on the board and instructed the children to add any answers they had not thought of to their list. The teacher continued noting the children's answers until they ran out of new suggestions.

The strategy was used again to get children to identify five 'healthy' or 'unhealthy' foods (and to give reasons for their answers). This led into a discussion of the various food groups, which was followed by a worksheet activity in which groups of children sorted foods into their appropriate food groups. The lesson ended with the teacher asking each child to write five sentences about healthy eating.

Almost all children were able to think of at least five answers to each of the questions. They responded well to the rapid pace of the lesson, and their level of involvement was high throughout the lesson.

The teachers have also introduced **Mixed Gender Pairing** to encourage boys and girls to work together (which they are unwilling to do, if the choice of work partner is left up to them). This strategy aims to break down the children's tendency to distract one another and to misbehave while working with children of the same gender. It is hoped that the children will learn from one another: for example, girls may benefit from the boys' tendency to work at a faster pace, and boys may benefit from seeing how girls pay attention to the presentation of their work.

Teachers allocate the children to their pairs, and paired work is planned for part of most lessons. The teacher ensures that the pairs are rotated, so that children are regularly paired with someone new. Depending on the activity, children are either paired with others of the same ability or in mixed-ability pairs.

Are the strategies successful?

The pilot stage of the initiative was evaluated through feedback sessions with the Year 6 class teachers. At St George's, the teacher felt that several of the strategies had proved successful, and this led to the use of these strategies throughout the school.

The KS2 teachers felt that, as a result of the strategies, relationships between boys and girls had improved considerably,

as had the behaviour of boys. Staff had noticed that boys and girls now cooperated better in class and were willing to play together in the playground. The children we spoke to had strongly positive views of two of the strategies (Circle Time and Going for Five) but had mixed views about the third (Mixed Gender Pairing).

You can discuss things, like when people say they're not friends [with other children], it can be sorted out.

Teachers felt that **Circle Time** had enabled all children to participate on an equal footing. Whereas previous class discussions tended to be dominated by boys shouting

out their opinions, the simple rules of the technique mean that boys are now willing to wait their turn and listen to the views of others in the class. It also contributes to a feeling of social cohesion within the class and encourages boys to express their feelings about personal and social issues, without fearing ridicule from their classmates. These points were echoed in the comments of the children we spoke to. One of the Year 5 boys said he liked Circle Time because: *'It's interesting finding out what others think';* and another commented: *'You can discuss things, like when people say they're not friends [with other children], it can be sorted out.'*

The teachers felt that **Going for Five** had improved children's motivation: they noticed that all children seemed to respond positively to the challenge of finding five answers in a short period of time, regardless of their gender or ability. Teachers found that they were able to cover a greater quantity of material more quickly. The structure of the technique stimulated group discussion, and gave the teacher the opportunity to encourage boys and girls of all abilities to participate. Teachers liked the fact that children were more actively involved in their own learning, rather than relying on the teacher for 'chalk and talk'.

A Year 6 boy explained that he liked the clear objectives and short deadlines involved in Going for

Five: *'If Miss says think of five things, then you know what you've got to get to in five minutes. But if you don't, then you might have two, and ten minutes have gone.'* One of the Year 6 girls suggested that because this technique placed responsibility on the children to think for themselves, it would be a useful preparation for secondary school: *'When you're going to the high school, the teachers aren't going to be telling you all these things, you're going to have to be finding them out for yourself; and I think Miss is trying to get us used to that.'*

> ## *You can get work done quicker if you sit next to a boy because they won't chat to you and you won't chat to them.*

Teachers felt that **Mixed Gender Pairing** helped to improve communication between the sexes and had a positive impact on girls' speed of task completion and boys' standard of work. As one teacher commented: *'The boys' presentation has improved because the girls won't accept untidy work.'* Few of the children we spoke to admitted to enjoying working with children of the opposite sex. As one Year 5 boy said: *'I think girls like to be next to a girl, and boys with a boy'*, and another complained: *'Girls copy and they start nagging.'* However

the children did recognise the positive effect of this strategy on their concentration. For example, one Year 6 boy said: *'If you're all boys then you'd probably not be talking about your work, you'd be talking about something else; and if you're all girls you might mess around, but when you're put into boy/girl groups you don't mess around as much.'* Similarly, a Year 6 girl said: *'You can get work done quicker if you sit next to a boy because they won't chat to you and you won't chat to them.'*

Although staff were convinced of the value of their project for pupils of both sexes they did not have any 'hard' evidence of its impact on attainment. They pointed out that the KS2 National Curriculum assessment results had improved by about 30 per cent after the first year of the project, but felt that it was not possible to attribute this to the implementation of the strategies alone. The school has identified the need to collect more

detailed information on pupils' progress in future. One of the school's targets is to implement a more thorough assessment system, which will enable teachers to track the progress of individual pupils throughout their time at the school.

Teachers were able to identify few disadvantages to their strategies, although they admitted that there was some additional work involved. This was due to the extra time spent planning how to integrate the new strategies into their teaching and also because the strategies (particularly Going for Five) enabled more work to be covered, which produced a greater amount of marking for staff.

What makes them work?

In this case, a group of schools identified a common problem and devised an initiative to address it. They benefited from the support of the LEA and were fortunate in finding someone with considerable expertise in the area, who was able to offer training and advice. The headteachers showed their commitment to the project by participating in the first training session. They decided to trial a range of strategies as part of a pilot phase, and considered which strategies were best suited to each school before spreading the initiative more widely in the second year.

At St George's, the strategies chosen were relatively easy for teachers to integrate with their normal classroom teaching. Teachers liked the fact that all three strategies are suitable for use across the curriculum and for children of all abilities. The strategies have been implemented flexibly. Teachers use them in different curriculum areas and at different frequencies according to the task and the characteristics of the pupils. For example, one teacher said she used Circle Time very rarely because one of the children in her class became particularly disruptive during it, while another teacher held Circle Time sessions three times a week.

Main advantages of this strategy

For pupils

- Overall, the strategies have led to an improvement in the relationship between boys and girls. Behaviour has improved and there is a better sense of cohesion within each class.

- **Circle Time** gives all children the opportunity to speak while others listen. It allows pupils to become more aware of their own views and feelings as well as the feelings of others.

- **Going for Five** helps children to consider alternative answers to problems and questions. Lessons have a more rapid pace and children can achieve short-term goals, which increases levels of interest and motivation. Children of all abilities are actively involved and are able to contribute.

- **Mixed Gender Pairing** encourages children to concentrate on their work and helps them learn to cooperate with others.

For teachers

- The strategies have provided teachers with new ways to approach their teaching. Children have become more motivated and are more willing to cooperate with one another.

- **Circle Time** enables teachers to explore personal and social issues with their classes. It reduces the domination of boys during class discussions, ensures that quieter, less confident children have an opportunity to contribute and improves the social cohesion of the class.

- **Going for Five** increases the pace of the lesson, children cover more material and levels of concentration are improved. It enables teachers to set a common task for the whole class, which can be differentiated by outcome (i.e. in the quantity and quality of pupils' responses).

- **Mixed Gender Pairing** reduces children's opportunities for becoming distracted and contributes towards improvements in girls' speed of response and boys' standards of presentation.

For the school

- This project has enabled staff from St George's to work together with neighbouring schools to address concerns about boys' underachievement.

Main disadvantages

○ Teachers have experienced a slightly increased workload, because of additional time spent in planning and marking work.

References

MacDONALD, A., SAUNDERS, L. and BENEFIELD, P. (1999). *Boys' Achievement, Progress, Motivation and Participation: Issues Raised by the Recent Literature.* Slough: NFER.

QUALIFICATIONS AND CURRICULUM AUTHORITY (1998b). *Standards at Key Stage 2: English, Mathematics and Science. Report on the 1998 National Curriculum Assessments for 11-year-olds. A Report for Headteachers, Teachers and Assessment Coordinators.* London: QCA.

Further reading on raising boys' achievement

ARNOT, M., GRAY, J., JAMES, M. and RUDDUCK, J. with DUVEEN, G. (1998). *Recent Research on Gender and Educational Performance* (OFSTED Reviews of Research). London: The Stationery Office.

BLEACH, K. (Ed) (1998). *Raising Boys' Achievement in Schools.* Stoke on Trent: Trentham Books.

MacDONALD, A., SAUNDERS, L. and BENEFIELD, P. (1999). *Boys' Achievement, Progress, Motivation and Participation: Issues Raised by the Recent Literature.* Slough: NFER.

QUALIFICATIONS AND CURRICULUM AUTHORITY (1998). *Can Do Better: Raising Boys' Achievement in English.* London: QCA.

PICKERING, J. (1997). *Raising Boys' Achievement* (School Effectiveness Series). Stafford: Network Educational Press.

Further reading on cooperative learning and group development

BLISS, T., ROBINSON, G. and MAINES, B. (1998). *Developing Circle Time.* London: Lucky Duck Publishing.

Raising Achievement in Reading and Improving Boys' Behaviour

In order to tackle children's underachievement in English, Langdon Road School has introduced a programme of 'paired reading'. Children in Year 4 are paired with children in Year 2. The initiative is intended to improve children's reading and to provide the younger boys, in particular, with positive role models. The school has also introduced initiatives to improve children's behaviour and social skills.

Introduction

For several years, it has been recognised that boys are underachieving at school. Results of KS2 National Curriculum assessments confirm that boys are continuing to fall behind girls in English, with particular weaknesses in reading and writing (OFSTED, 1999a; MacDonald *et al.*, 1999). It has been suggested that one of the reasons for this is a lack of male role models: mothers are more likely than fathers to read with their children and the majority of primary teachers are women. As a result, boys may come to view reading as an essentially 'female' activity.

Paired reading is a structured method for helping children to read. A recent review of strategies to help poor readers concluded that paired reading approaches are an effective means of improving reading skills, provided that training is given (Brooks *et al.*, 1998). Research into the use of same-gender, as opposed to mixed-gender pairings for shared reading found that boys made particularly good progress when working in same-gender pairs (Topping and Whiteley, 1993).

About the school

Langdon Road School is situated in a small town. There are 188 children on the school's roll, from nursery to Year 4. Historically, local employers have provided work in heavy industry. Now, however, the children come from a range of different social backgrounds. Many parents work in local banks, shops or in manual jobs, but there are also some families where one or both parents are unemployed. A small number come from ethnic minority backgrounds. About 30 per cent of the children are entitled to free school meals and 22 per cent are on the special needs register.

The development of the strategy

When the head joined the school in 1996, she was concerned that the children were not performing up to the local or national averages, particularly in English. To identify the reasons for this, the head and the staff examined the children's National Curriculum English assessment papers, focusing on the questions that children had been unable to answer. This exercise revealed that many children were capable of achieving a higher grade, but had just missed out. According to the head: *'The key for our children was vocabulary and we also noticed their habit of communicating in very simple language, using short sentences.'* The staff felt a strategy was needed which would improve reading, expand the children's vocabulary and develop their communication skills.

The head was particularly concerned about the underachievement of boys in the school and had noticed that an anti-learning culture seemed to be perpetuated amongst them. For example, there was a group of boys in Year 4 who were *'football players, tough guys, for whom learning wasn't particularly cool'.*

The school's interest in these issues coincided with an LEA initiative on raising boys' achievement. The LEA had developed a video for children on the subject of paired reading, which the school used to introduce the idea to teachers and pupils. The paired reading technique can be used with same-age or cross-age groups. The staff thought that asking boys in Year 4 to tutor younger boys would encourage the older boys to develop their social skills and become more considerate of others' feelings. They hoped that it would benefit the younger boys to see the older ones in a new light, in an educational setting, rather than as the dominant presence in the playground.

At the same time, the school introduced personal and social education lessons to tackle some of the issues relating to poor behaviour. They used drama to help children widen their vocabulary and expressive language, and to develop children's self-confidence.

The strategy

Paired reading was first introduced into the school in 1996. It takes place during a 20-minute period, three times a week. At any one time, eight children from Year 4 are paired with eight from Year 2. Both boys and girls take part, in same-gender pairs. Four pairs sit in the Year 2 classroom and the other four sit in the Year 4 classroom. They read together while the rest of their classes read individually. After working together for six weeks, another eight children are chosen to participate.

Before the Year 4 children begin the paired reading, they watch the LEA video, which gives them suggestions about the different

ways they can read with the younger children (such as: alone, with the younger child listening; together; or with the older child listening to the younger child read). It also provides prompts for children to use with their partner. These include: 'Have you discussed the pictures?', 'Have you asked questions?', 'Have you discussed the story?', and 'Have you looked for new words or sounds?'

During the paired reading session, the Year 2 child chooses the book that they will read and the children decide who will read out loud. The Year 4 child is responsible for asking their partner questions about different words in the book, the story, the characters and the pictures. They are also required to write a comment on their partner's progress after each session on a specially designed form. From time to time, staff check that the children are taking it in turns to read to one another.

The costs incurred in setting up and running the paired reading sessions were relatively small. The school had bought the training video from the LEA, at a cost of around £12. The only other cost was for more reading books, so that the children had a wider selection to choose from for the paired reading sessions.

Is it successful?

The head said that one of the main benefits of the paired reading sessions was the confidence it gives the children, particularly the older children who act as tutors. She commented that both boys and girls had benefited from the scheme, but that the staff had noticed a strong impact on the older boys, who enjoyed taking on a responsible role.

It used to be too quick but I have had to slow it down so that the younger children can understand.

Teachers gave examples of how the scheme had helped individual children. For example, one Year 4 girl who took part in the paired reading was extremely shy and cried a lot at school. This girl gained in confidence through the scheme and became *'one of the best tutors we have ever had'*. Similarly a boy with behavioural difficulties acted very responsibly as a tutor, and gained pride in his ability to help a younger child. The Year 4 class teacher noticed the positive effects of the scheme on the children in her class: *'It helps them with their own reading as it gives them something to aim for, gives them a bit of pride in themselves.'*

The children we interviewed echoed these sentiments. One Year 4 child said that she felt *'grown-up, filling in the shared reading forms'*. Another explained how she had changed her method of reading aloud to accommodate the needs of the younger child: *'It used to be too quick but I have had to slow it down so that the younger children can understand.'* The children felt that the scheme had helped their reading skills. One commented:

'My vocabulary has improved', and another said *'We become better readers.'*

After each six-week block, the children are asked if they have enjoyed the paired reading sessions. The Year 4 children write their answers on an evaluation sheet, while the younger children are asked the same questions orally by the head. Questions include: whether they have enjoyed paired reading; whether both partners have read to one another; whether they have noticed any changes in their partner's reading; and whether they now feel more confident in reading out loud. The results of these evaluations have been very positive: the pupils say they enjoy taking part in the scheme and both age-groups benefit.

Staff feel that the paired reading, together with the focus on positive behaviour in drama and PSE lessons, has had a positive impact on behaviour throughout the school. There is now very little bullying, and relationships between pupils and teachers have improved. This was confirmed by the school's 1998 inspection report, which commented favourably on the quality of pupils' relationships and standards of behaviour. *'The school has a very good ethos which promotes equal opportunities for all pupils. Under the leadership of the headteacher the school has already achieved significant improvement in the standards attained. ... Relationships at all levels are good ... Although pupils are restricted to a crowded and awkwardly shaped, sloping playground, there is no rough play and they are considerate of each other. We observed no bullying or*

name calling and pupils commented that there is none.'

The children's reading scores have been monitored, to see whether the paired reading is having any impact on attainment. Results of standardised reading tests in Year 4 indicated that over the first two terms of the paired reading initiative, the 24 participating children improved their reading ages by an average of 13 months. This compared with an average gain of five months for the rest of the class. Six of the children who took part in the paired reading initiative increased their reading ages by more than two years (one of whom increased his reading score by 4.6 years in seven months).

Key Stage 1 results for reading have also shown an improvement. Although the school is still below local and national averages, the annual scores have shown consistent increases (from 45 per cent achieving Level 2 or more in 1995, to 77 per cent achieving Level 2 or more in 1998). However, as the school also introduced a new reading scheme at about the same time, the head felt that it was impossible to attribute these improvements to the impact of the paired reading initiative alone.

The main difficulty that the staff encountered with the paired reading scheme was ensuring that every child had a partner of the same gender. (This was an important feature of the initiative, because the intention was to provide younger boys with positive male role models.) In one Year 2 group, there were very few boys with whom the Year 4s could be paired. As a result, it was not possible to place all the children in same-gender pairs. In addition, teachers said it was sometimes difficult to devote attention to supervising the paired reading sessions while dealing with the rest of the class. As one teacher pointed out: *'It would be lovely if we had an extra adult to supervise it.'*

What makes it work?

This school had identified a weakness in reading, and staff were concerned about the behaviour and attitudes of boys. The staff discussed the issues and decided to use an LEA scheme to help improve reading. They made the decision to use same-gender and cross-age pairs to strengthen the potential positive effects on boys.

Teachers felt that it is important to ensure that all children have a chance to participate in the shared reading, because they are aware of the potential damage to the self-esteem of any child who is left out. The choice of pairs is a key element in the success of the strategy, as the Year 4 class teacher explained: *'We try to pair the Year 2 children with someone who is a slightly better reader than them. You've got to compare personalities as well: you don't put two silly boys together...and you don't want the younger child to be too dominated by the older child.'* Staff recognised the need to work on some children's interpersonal skills before involving them in the project. As the head remarked: *'If you ask a child to be a tutor for the shared reading and he is a bully in the playground, you have to work on his social skills as well.'*

If you ask a child to be a tutor for the shared reading and he is a bully in the playground, you have to work on his social skills as well.

The school has adjusted their scheme in response to the children's reactions. For example, when the strategy was first introduced, all the children in Years 2 and 4 took part in the paired reading sessions for a whole year. However, the children's comments indicated that their enthusiasm faded over such a long period, so it was decided to limit the time to a six-week period. In future, the school plans to introduce individual target setting, which will link in with the paired reading scheme.

Main advantages of this strategy

For the older pupils

- Satisfaction is gained from helping younger children to read.

- A greater sense of responsibility is developed.

- Reading and communication skills improve as they tutor the younger children.

- They gain an understanding of the way children learn to read which, in turn, can help them with their own reading.

For the younger pupils

- Positive male role models are provided and, as a result, there is less pressure for boys to conform to traditional 'macho' stereotypes.

- The individual attention helps them to develop their reading skills.

For all pupils

- Ability to read aloud improves, and their vocabulary widens.

- Paired reading fosters positive relationships between older and younger children.

- As a result of several initiatives on improving behaviour, there has been a reduction in the level of physical and verbal bullying in the playground.

For teachers

- They know that during the paired reading sessions, a number of children in their class will be receiving individual attention.

- Paired reading reinforces work on social skills covered in PSE lessons.

- Teachers spend less time managing behaviour and resolving disputes between pupils.

For the school

- Paired reading, together with other initiatives, has contributed to improved attainment in reading and to a positive school ethos. These aspects were noted in the school's OFSTED inspection report.

- As a result of several initiatives on reading, Key Stage 1 results have improved, as have Year 4 reading scores.

Main disadvantages

- Without additional help, it is difficult for teachers to give sufficient attention to the paired readers while supervising the rest of the class.

References

BROOKS, G., FLANAGAN, N., HENKHUZENS, Z. and HUTCHISON, D. (1998). *What Works for Slow Readers? The Effectiveness of Early Intervention Schemes.* Slough: NFER.

MacDONALD, A., SAUNDERS, L. and BENEFIELD, P. (1999). *Boys' Achievement, Progress, Motivation and Participation: Issues Raised by the Recent Literature.* Slough: NFER.

OFFICE FOR STANDARDS IN EDUCATION (1999a). *The Annual Report of Her Majesty's Chief Inspector of Schools: Standards and Quality in Education 1997/98.* London: OFSTED.

TOPPING, K. and WHITELEY, M. (1993). 'Sex differences in the effectiveness of peer tutoring', *School Psychology International*, **14**, 1, 57-67.

Further reading on literacy and paired reading

BROOKS, G., FLANAGAN, N., HENKHUZENS, Z. and HUTCHISON, D. (1998). *What Works for Slow Readers? The Effectiveness of Early Intervention Schemes.* Slough: NFER.

TOPPING, K. (1995). *Paired Reading, Spelling and Writing: the Handbook for Teachers and Parents.* London: Cassell.

Further reading on raising boys' achievement

ARNOT, M., GRAY, J., JAMES, M. and RUDDUCK, J. with DUVEEN, G. (1998). *Recent Research on Gender and Educational Performance* (OFSTED Reviews of Research). London: The Stationery Office.

BLEACH, K. (Ed) (1998). *Raising Boys' Achievement in Schools.* Stoke on Trent: Trentham Books.

MacDONALD, A., SAUNDERS, L. and BENEFIELD, P. (1999). *Boys' Achievement, Progress, Motivation and Participation: Issues Raised by the Recent Literature.* Slough: NFER.

QUALIFICATIONS AND CURRICULUM AUTHORITY (1998). *Can Do Better: Raising Boys' Achievement in English.* London: QCA.

PICKERING, J. (1997). *Raising Boys' Achievement* (School Effectiveness Series). Stafford: Network Educational Press.

Further reading on discipline and behaviour

DOCKING, J. (1996). *Managing Behaviour in the Primary School.* 2nd edn. London: David Fulton.

WATKINS, C. (1997). M*anaging Classroom Behaviour: a Bit Like Air Traffic Control.* London: Association of Teachers and Lecturers.

Individual Target Setting and Developing Key Skills

Chadsmead Primary School is one of seven schools in their LEA to have piloted Primary Planners with children in Years 5 and 6. Primary Planners are an individual planning diary for children, in which they can provide feedback to teachers about their learning experiences and set their own targets for the development of key skills.

Introduction

It has long been recognised that children need to develop a number of 'core' or 'key' transferable skills, which make a vital contribution to educational and personal development and ultimately to a young person's employability.

The precise definition of key skills has varied over the years. However, following Sir Ron Dearing's review of the post-16 curriculum, six key skill areas have been identified: communication; application of number; information technology; working with others; improving own learning and performance; and problem solving (see QCA, 1998a).

Because key skills are not the province of specific curriculum areas, schools need to ensure that children are given specific opportunities to develop them. Although it is intended that key skills should be developed throughout a child's education, much of the attention has been

focused on secondary schooling, particularly post-16. The LEA initiative described here is therefore somewhat unusual, because it concerns primary pupils.

About the school

Chadsmead Primary School is situated in a large village bordering a city. There are 213 children on roll, aged four to 11. Chadsmead serves a multicultural population, taking children of 14 different nationalities (several of whom speak English as an additional language). The school is located near to a university, and over a third of the children have parents in professional employment. The school has a low proportion of pupils eligible for free school meals and accommodates relatively few children with special educational needs.

The development of the strategy

Primary Planners grew out of work by an educational consultant on the use of homework diaries in secondary schools. The project demonstrated that homework diaries were a valuable means of enhancing communication between teachers and parents. In order to develop the initiative further, the LEA held a conference to explore the possibility of adapting homework diaries to help upper primary pupils develop key skills. Chadsmead was one of seven schools chosen to pilot the initiative for a two-year period. The LEA allocated a budget of £6,000 to fund the pilot stage. Following the success of the first year of the pilot, the scheme has expanded to include over 40 primary schools throughout the LEA.

The seven pilot schools each appointed a coordinator who had responsibility for implementing the strategy and liasing with a planning team (made up of the coordinators from the seven pilot schools and an LEA representative). Team meetings took place once a term, and the planning team organised annual conferences to share information with colleagues in other schools. The team also developed a set of guidelines for use by schools wishing to join the scheme.

Staff in Chadsmead Primary School welcomed the opportunity to take part in the early stages of this initiative, seeing it as a means of developing children's skills, enhancing their self-esteem and raising achievement.

The strategy

The Primary Planner is an A5 document with a spiral binding and laminated covers. It is in two main sections: a section on key skills and a diary/weekly planner. The Planner also contains printed information on term dates and school dress and there is an outline timetable, a section for pupils to write down spellings and space for personal notes.

The key skills section aims to help children evaluate their existing skills and set longer-term targets for improvement. Five key skill areas are identified: communication; application of number; information technology; problem solving; and personal skills. Each skill area is broken down into up to 15 statements, listed on the left-hand page. For example, one of the statements listed under the key skill of

Communication reads: 'I can explain things to people', and another says: 'I can ask questions and answer questions in class'. Children assess their progress in relation to each statement using a five-point scale (1 = 'can't do or no experience', 5 = 'confident'). The following pages invite children to write in their comments under three headings: 'Examples which show I have used these skills:', 'I need to improve on:' and 'I can do this by:'.

The diary takes up the main part of the Planner. Each two-page spread lists the days of the week, with space for notes. At the beginning of the week, children are invited to write in a target to achieve ('This week I will...'). At the end, there is a review section where children are asked to note 'The thing I have been really proud of this week' and 'The most difficult thing I have done this week', and are invited to set a target for the following week. There is space for a comment and a signature from a parent or guardian.

Each school decides how best to make use of the Planners. At Chadsmead, teachers try to give pupils time each day to write down their impressions of lessons in the diary section of their Planner. Children are encouraged to write evaluative comments: not just what happened in the lesson, but how they reacted to the teaching and how well they understood the topic. Children also make a note of their homework and can include any messages their teachers wish to convey to parents. Parents are asked to sign the Planner each week, after discussing it with their child.

The Planners are collected periodically by teachers. This allows teachers to read the comments, and to check that pupils' targets are realistic and achievable. Each term, teachers hold a session for children to review their key skills. Children evaluate their progress so far and set themselves new targets for the future. They are encouraged to ask for help from teachers and parents to identify ways in which they can develop their skills.

O/Autumn   O/Summer
O/Spring

COMMUNICATION SKILLS

	Confident	Can Do	Manage	Difficult	Can't Do No Experience
I can spell and use words correctly	1	(2)	3	4	5
I know the meaning of words	1	(2)	(3)	4	5
I can read and understand	(1)	2	3	4	5
I can write letters and creative stories	(1)	2	3	4	5
I can use punctuations, Capital Letters, paragraphs etc.	1	(2)	(3)	4	5
I can explain things to people	1	(2)	(3)	4	5
I can speak in formal situations eg. to a group, in assembly	1	(2)	3	4	5
I can act as spokesperson for a group	1	(2)	3	4	5
I can ask questions and answer questions in class	1	(2)	(3)	4	5
I can put forward my own point of view	1	(2)	3	4	5
I can give directions to a visitor	1	(2)	(3)	4	5
I can listen to others and follow what they are saying	1	(2)	(3)	4	5
I can listen to and follow instructions	1	(2)	(3)	4	5
I can use the telephone	(1)	(2)	3	4	5
My handwriting is neat and easy for others to read.	(1)	(2)	3	4	5

Examples which show that I have used these skills:

I did apostrophes and I did Capital Letters in my work. I went up in special mention it was good.

I need to improve on: Speaking in a big group in front assembly. Putting forward my point of view. achieved

I can do this by: Try harder at work to go in special mention and talk about what I have done. Being more confident

Is it successful?

In order to evaluate the success of the Planners, questionnaires were sent to headteachers, class teachers, pupils, parents and governors in the seven pilot schools. The responses to the questionnaires showed that most of those involved held very positive views about the usefulness of the Planners.

The teachers, pupils and parents we spoke to agreed that the Planners had a number of benefits, including helping children to organise their work. According to the children we spoke to, the fact that important information is stored together, just as in a personal organiser, is one of the Planner's best features. As one Year 6 pupil said: *'It organises you a bit more and makes you try harder.'* Similarly, a teacher commented: *'The Planners are great as an organisational tool.'*

It organises you a bit more and makes you try harder.

Parents were able to identify several examples of the way in which the Planners had helped their children. A parent governor explained: *'My daughter is a perfectionist; she takes her time to do a piece of work and she wasn't getting things finished. This came out in the Planner [so] with an action plan she's speeded herself up and is completing tasks on time.'* Another parent commented on how the Planners can be used to build up self-esteem: *'Every child can think of something they have been proud of in the week.'* The Planners also provide parents with information about what their child is doing at school. As one pupil explained: *'When you come home and your mum asks you what you have done at school instead of saying "Oh nothing", you can give her your Planner and she can look at it.'*

The teachers discuss any general issues identified in the Planners as part of their school development planning. The head explained that one of the school's current areas for development had originated in this way: *'Through discussion with groups of children, we identified a need to develop the playground. Children commented in their Planners that they found lunchtime lengthy and were aware that our school grounds could be utilised to better effect. This all came out of the Primary Planners.'*

What makes it work?

One of the key characteristics of this strategy is that it is part of an LEA initiative. The LEA committed resources to the project, and provided support for review and development during a pilot phase. According to the LEA adviser we spoke to, the demand from other primary schools to join the initiative is a testament to the popularity of the idea.

Chadsmead staff believed that the strategy worked well in their school because they had adopted a whole-school approach. All the staff, as well as the parents and governors, were involved in the process. The fact that the initiative offered added value without taking up too much staff time was seen to be an advantage. As one teacher pointed out, Planners could be *'combined with the curriculum without having to push anything else to one side'*.

Staff recognised that children need to build up their self-evaluation skills over time. They noted that,

while pupils begin by writing purely descriptive comments, their ability to evaluate their experiences and to set targets develops with support from teachers and parents. Year 6 pupils, who have been using the Planners for a year, are much more skilled in this respect. Of course, individuals differ in their ability to use their Planners to best effect. Some children are reluctant to write anything that they feel is too personal or to be critical of teachers because they are afraid of what teachers and parents will think when they read it. Both teachers and pupils recognised that whilst most children were very conscientious and proud of their Planner, a few experience completing their Planners as something of a chore. Ultimately, the success of the Planners is dependent on the willingness of pupils, teachers and parents to realise the potential of this self-evaluation and organisational tool.

Every child can think of something they have been proud of in the week.

In order to get the maximum benefits from using the Planners, staff have made adjustments to the way they are used. For example, teachers found that it worked better to review the key skill targets once, rather than twice a term. One teacher decided to let her pupils know what they would be covering in class at the beginning of each term, so they could set relevant targets according to the topics. Another

allocated a regular weekly period of 30 – 40 minutes for children to focus on their Planners, instead of slotting the Planners into the day whenever she had the time.

During the pilot phase, the content of the Planners had been modified in a number of ways, including moving the Key Skills section from the back to the front of the Planner in order to emphasise its importance and adding a section to help children transferring to secondary school ('Things I need to know before moving to my next school').

When we asked the pupils if there was anything they would like to see improved, they said they would like more attention to be paid to the presentation of the Planner in order to enhance its status as a personal organiser (e.g. by adding coloured printing and by producing them in an A5 ring binder).

Postscript

Since our visit to the school, the initiative has developed still further. The Planner now looks more like a personal organiser and is presented in an A5 ring binder. All primary schools in the authority are using Planners with Years 5 and 6. A secondary version has been developed for Years 7 and 8, and simpler versions are being devised for Years 3/4 and 1/2. A working group is developing a good practice guide and a software program has been commissioned to help children to summarise their key skills and other achievements at the end of Year 6. This 'transfer document' is being trialled by a group of 20 primary and secondary schools.

Main advantages of this strategy

For pupils

- The Planners help children to organise their learning, which contributes to improvements in responsibility and independence.

- Primary Planners provide children with a record of what they have done at school.

- They help children to identify their successes in relation to key skills, which enhances their self-esteem. Children become aware of their weaknesses and can plan to address them.

- They provide children with a channel through which to express themselves and to communicate things to adults that they may be reluctant to say out loud.

- The development of Year 6/7 Planners should help ease the transition between primary and secondary school.

For teachers

- Primary Planners provide opportunities for teachers to address children's individual learning needs.

- The Planners provide teachers with an insight into how children feel about different teaching methods and activities. Teachers can use pupils' feedback in planning future activities with their class.

- The Planners provide an effective means of communicating with parents.

For the school

- Primary Planners enable the school to focus on the development of key skills.

- Primary Planners are a flexible tool that can be related to all areas of the curriculum.

- They help the school to involve parents in their children's learning.

- They provide a good opportunity to review pupils' progress on a regular basis.

- Issues raised by children can be addressed as part of the school's development planning.

For parents

- Primary Planners provide parents with an insight into what their children are doing at school.

- They give parents the opportunity to see how their children perceive themselves and how they progress over time. Parents can help their children to achieve their learning goals.

- The Planners provide a means of communication between parents and teachers.

For the LEA

- This initiative is aimed at developing key skills throughout primary and secondary education, helping to fulfil the LEA's commitment to lifelong learning.

- The pilot phase allowed the Planners to be fully trialled and adapted for use in primary schools. The conferences provided opportunities for teachers to discuss the initiative with practitioners in other schools, and to persuade them of the benefits of the initiative.

- It is hoped that the development of Year 6/7 Planners will help the LEA to address the potential problem of a drop in pupils' attainment during the period of transfer to secondary school.

Main disadvantages

- Planners take time for pupils to complete and for teachers and parents to read.

Reference

QUALIFICATIONS AND CURRICULUM AUTHORITY (1998a). *Qualifying for Success: Report on the Consultation about the Future of Post-16 Qualifications.* London: QCA.

Further reading on transition between primary and secondary school

QUALIFICATIONS AND CURRICULUM AUTHORITY (1998). *Building Bridges: Guidance and Training Materials for Teachers of Year 6 and Year 7 Pupils.* London: QCA.

Using Group Work to Develop Social and Evaluation Skills

Waterbeach Junior School has introduced a programme of group work to enable children to develop social and evaluation skills and as a method of improving children's behaviour at school.

Introduction

The development of key skills such as communication, working with others, problem-solving and improving one's own learning and performance are essential if young people are to be able to cooperate successfully with others. Children who develop these skills at school are more likely to be effective learners and valuable employees (QCA, 1998a). However, it is not always easy for primary teachers to find ways of introducing key skills into their everyday teaching.

The basic idea behind cooperative group work is that it encourages children to collaborate to complete a shared task, rather than working individually or competitively. There is a variety of techniques and activities available to teachers wishing to introduce cooperative group work. These range from whole-class activities to tasks set for groups or pairs. Supporters of cooperative learning suggest that it can promote positive relationships through valuing individual diversity, encouraging active participation and enabling children to resolve conflict. It is argued that group work helps children to develop self-esteem, promotes social skills and

motivates children. There is also some evidence from research in the USA that the use of cooperative group techniques can lead to significant gains in children's academic achievement (Bossert, 1988; Johnson and Johnson, 1994).

About the school

Waterbeach Junior School is situated on the outskirts of a large coastal town. It has a mixed catchment area, including a women's refuge and council estates as well as privately owned accommodation. Thirteen per cent of the children are eligible for free school meals. Most of the children are white, although a few of them come from Chinese, African and Asian families. The school accommodates 408 children in 12 classes from Year 4 to Year 6. There are 14 full-time and five part-time teaching staff (16.5 FTE).

The development of the strategy

Waterbeach staff have been interested in developing their assessment techniques for many years. They felt confident in assessing the *outcomes* of children's work but were having problems finding the time to assess the processes that children used in their work. They wanted to help children develop skills of self-evaluation.

There was an increasing problem

of poor behaviour among new entrants to the school. The establishment of the refuge and increasing competition from private schools meant that the school's intake was changing in social and academic terms. Staff felt that they were spending too much time disciplining pupils and intervening in playground disputes.

These two issues were discussed at a staff meeting in the autumn of 1993. One member of staff was familiar with the aims and processes involved in collaborative group work because he had chosen to study it as part of his BEd degree. He suggested that collaborative group work could offer a way forward. The rest of the staff felt that this could be a useful way of encouraging children to develop evaluation, communication and teamwork skills. They hoped that collaborative group work would improve children's behaviour by strengthening social skills and establishing positive relationships among children and between children and teachers.

Teachers set up a working group to consider the most effective way of introducing collaborative group techniques. The working group comprised the teacher who had suggested the idea, together with the deputy head and a teacher from each year-group. Funding from the school's INSET budget was used to pay for supply cover to enable the group to meet during school time. The working group looked at a variety of activities designed to encourage group work, and considered which ones were the most beneficial and easiest to introduce. They also outlined a plan for the introduction of group work, so that children's skills could be developed over time. The first stage was to help children to 'orientate' themselves within the class and to get to know one another at the beginning of the school year. A programme of activities designed to help children to develop and refine their collaborative and evaluation skills would follow.

The conclusions of the working group were presented to the whole staff and everyone agreed to try out various collaborative group activities at the beginning of the next academic year. The working group put together an action plan, which was accompanied by a resource pack of activities together with specific performance indicators and suggested evaluation strategies. The deputy head videotaped some group work in her own class and visited other classes to demonstrate group techniques while the class teacher observed.

The strategy

At Waterbeach, children are regrouped into classes every year. This is done to break down existing groups to some extent and to help children to relate to new people. The first week of the new year is organised to promote cohesion within the new classes through Circle Time and other group activities (for example, children are asked to complete a short questionnaire about their classmates and then to share the resulting information with the class).

During the rest of the year, group development work is used frequently in physical education lessons (taught by the deputy head) and in other subjects, at the discretion of the class teacher. As part of the group work, children are encouraged to assess their

strengths and weaknesses and to provide feedback to each other about how their work could be improved. This is shown in the following example.

The teachers choose when to use group development techniques throughout the year, and some teachers used them more extensively than others. For example, a Year 4 teacher described how he had set group tasks in a variety of subjects. In science, children collaborated to design a 'phases of the moon' game, and in music, groups of children worked on a 'planet suite' composition.

In the first year, the initiative cost £700 to set up, and a similar amount was spent in the second year. By the third year, the expenditure fell to £300, and its costs are now within the normal school budget.

Is it successful?

The staff introduced their chosen activities during the first two weeks of the autumn term and held a feedback meeting to discuss their experiences. Teachers and pupils enjoyed the

During our visit to the school, we observed a Year 6 dance lesson on the theme of 'a Victorian Christmas'. The lesson was led by the deputy head, who started by asking all the children to choose a partner. She played them a piece of music and asked them to mime the servants' preparations for Christmas in a large Victorian household. The teacher then divided the pairs into two groups and asked each group to perform to the other. The children in the audience were asked to give feedback to their partners on the quality of their mimes. Almost all children were able to identify features of the performance that they thought were particularly effective. The teacher then invited the children to comment on areas that could be improved (for example, one boy suggested that his partner could: *'Push with your whole hand, not just your fingertips'*). Constructive criticism was received well and the children put a great deal of effort into improving their mimes in the ways their partners suggested.

activities, and many of the targets set for the activities had been achieved, but some of the group work was disrupted by poor behaviour. A minority of children were unable to take turns, listen to others, or deal with conflicting views.

I like working together because if we have different ideas then we get to learn more.

In response to this problem, the teachers decided to focus on helping these children before introducing activities requiring a greater degree of collaboration. Children identified as having poor social skills worked in small groups with two teachers. The teachers encouraged them to reflect on their social behaviour. (For example, in one of the role-play exercises, children were asked to demonstrate how they would help someone who had dropped some packages.) The

sessions were videotaped and replayed to the children for comment. By watching the video recordings, children became more aware of the way in which their behaviour affected other people, and were able to consider how to modify their actions.

A new school behaviour policy was introduced at the same time. Teachers discussed the issue with their classes and helped the children to set some simple rules of behaviour that everyone agreed to uphold. Children were given responsibility for solving their own disputes, although they could call on a member of staff to mediate. Teachers held a staff meeting to examine the ways in which they dealt with discipline, and agreed to adopt a more consistent approach. A school council was established to discuss issues raised by pupils.

The staff we spoke to identified several positive social, personal and academic benefits arising from their initiatives. Teachers felt that the use of group development work at the beginning of each year helped them to get to know their new

classes, and encouraged a sense of group cohesion. The use of group work to develop children's key skills was felt to be successful, as the deputy head explained: *'If they [the children] have the skills to observe other children and the ability to discuss differences...they become more willing to try and improve and ... their self-esteem and confidence also grows.'* Staff felt that the group work has helped children's decision-making and that children were becoming increasingly able to work independently of the teacher.

Children felt that the group work had had a positive impact on their learning. As one Year 4 child said: *'I like working together because if we have different ideas then we get to learn more.'* They said that although they sometimes argued about what to did, they were usually able to resolve the problem by 'joining the ideas together'.

Children acknowledged that receiving criticism from their classmates could be difficult, but that feedback from other children was useful, as a Year 6 child explained: *'When other children say things, we know that they can help us because they have done it themselves.'* Children also felt that the cooperative group work had improved their relationships with others: *'If you get on together then we are one happy group and if the class did the same then we will be one happy class of friendship.'*

Staff felt that children's behaviour had improved as a result of the group work and behaviour policies. The head commented: *'We have found that the children are behaving better, they are more responsible... teachers are now able to spend more time teaching and less time managing behaviour.'*

Results in the three core subjects have improved each year since 1995. In 1998, 64 per cent of Year 6 children gained Level 4 or more in mathematics, 70 per cent in English and 82 per cent in science. The school thought the improvements were due to a combination of factors, including the group development work.

The school's 1997 OFSTED inspection report commented favourably on the social and learning effects of the school's group work.

'The "group development" programme which focuses on working together and building trust considerably enhances pupils' social development. It encourages a sense of community which pervades all aspects of school life and has a very positive effect on pupils' learning.'

The school's group development initiative has come to the attention of other schools. The LEA link adviser invited the head of Waterbeach to describe their use of group work at an INSET coordinators' meeting.

The positive OFSTED inspection report provided the school with an endorsement of their approach. Staff were planning to develop their use of collaborative group work in future, although they commented that pressure from Government initiatives (such as those in literacy, numeracy and ICT) has made it hard to find time

to focus on the school's own priorities.

The children are behaving better, they are more responsible... teachers are now able to spend more time teaching and less time managing behaviour.

Staff could identify few drawbacks with their initiative. However, the head commented that it had been difficult to fund the initiative entirely from school resources. Also, the group work had proved to be quite demanding on teachers, who are required to adopt the role of facilitator. Some teachers have found it more difficult than others to work in this way.

What makes it work?

In this school, the strategies have evolved over a number of years. The staff recognised that they needed to address the problem of deteriorating standards of behaviour. They also wanted to find a way of developing children's evaluation skills.

In order to address these issues, they drew on existing staff expertise. They set up a working group with members from each year-group. The head supported the initiative and agreed to devote school funding to enable staff to meet during school time. The working group's plan was clearly defined and was backed up with resources and support. The whole staff agreed to implement the initiative, and evaluated their experiences against clearly defined performance indicators. The evaluation revealed an unexpected problem: some children did not have the basic social skills to enable them to participate in group work. Rather

than abandoning the initiative altogether, teachers introduced behaviour and discipline policies, before taking their group work to the next stage. Despite their initial difficulties, all staff have continued with the first stage of the initiative and some have developed it further.

Main advantages of this strategy

For pupils

- The group activities at the beginning of the year help children to get to know their new teacher and classmates.

- Children's views are listened to and respected. Children learn to deal with conflict and to work with others.

- Children's confidence and self-esteem improve.

- They develop evaluation skills and learn to accept constructive criticism.

- Their decision-making improves, as does their ability to learn independently of the teacher.

- Working collaboratively in groups can be more enjoyable than completing individual tasks.

For teachers

- Teachers get to know their new classes at the beginning of the year and the cohesion of the class is improved.

- Children are more sociable and their evaluation skills are developed. They are able to work independently of the teacher.

- Teachers develop their own ability to act as a facilitator and resource for children's learning.

- The positive impact of the group work and behaviour policies means that teachers spend less time managing behaviour.

For the school

- Group work offers a means of developing children's key skills, such as communication, problem-solving, working with others and improving their own learning and performance.

- As a result of their group work initiative, the school has received positive feedback from OFSTED and recognition from the LEA.

- School becomes a calmer place as the children's social skills improve and they take responsibility for solving their own disputes.

Main disadvantages

- Some teachers find it difficult to adapt to the demands of group work.

References

BOSSERT, S.T. (1988). 'Cooperative activities in the classroom.' In: ROTHKOPF, E.Z. (Ed) *Review of Research in Education* 15: 1988-89. Washington, DC: American Educational Research Association.

QUALIFICATIONS AND CURRICULUM AUTHORITY (1998a). *Qualifying for Success: Report on the Consultation about the Future of Post-16 Qualifications.* London: QCA.

JOHNSON, D.W. and JOHNSON, R.T. (1994). 'Collaborative learning and argumentation.' In: KUTNICK, P. and ROGERS C. (Eds) *Groups in Schools.* London: Cassell.

Further reading on cooperative learning and groupwork

BLISS, T., ROBINSON, G. and MAINES, B. (1998). *Developing Circle Time*. London: Lucky Duck Publishing.

DUNNE, E. and BENNETT, N. (1990). *Talking and Learning in Groups: Activity Based In-service and Pre-service Materials* (Leverhulme Primary Project Classroom Skills Series). Basingstoke: MacMillan Education.

Further reading on discipline and behaviour

DOCKING, J. (1996). *Managing Behaviour in the Primary School.* 2nd edn. London: David Fulton.

WATKINS, C. (1997). *Managing Classroom Behaviour: a Bit Like Air Traffic Control.* London: Association of Teachers and Lecturers.

Raising Achievement in English Through Parental Involvement

Portland Primary School has involved parents in helping their own children to develop literacy skills at home. A group of parents also visit the school each week to help lower-attaining children with their basic skills.

Introduction

It has long been argued that parental support is a key element in children's success at school. Strong home–school links aid communication between teachers and parents, demonstrate parents' interest in their children's progress and enable school work to be reinforced outside the classroom. Research into approaches using parents to support children's learning has shown that these can raise achievement, providing that parents receive adequate guidance and training (Brooks *et al.*, 1998; Topping, 1995).

About the school

Portland Primary School is located on the outskirts of a major city. The area suffers from social deprivation: local unemployment rates are high and those parents who are in work are generally employed in low-paid, part-time jobs. Over half of the 300 children on the school's roll are entitled to free school meals, and a third are registered as having special educational needs. All of the children come from white backgrounds. The school has a nursery on site and there are ten

classes from reception to Year 6, including four mixed-age classes. There are 12 teaching staff and six classroom assistants.

The development of the strategy

The initiative was first developed in 1991 by the home–school liaison teacher. At the time, she was working for her Masters degree, and was interested in fostering closer links between parents and teachers. She contacted the authority's Community Education Officer and, together with the head, they decided to put together a bid to the local authority's community fund to set up a family literacy project

in the school, involving parents of nursery-age children.

The materials were developed by the home–school liaison teacher, based on work at Sheffield University. Staff started by developing stronger links with parents, through a series of home visits. The school devised a series of activities for parents to work on at home with their children. Parents were encouraged to attend a series of coffee mornings and basic skills workshops on themes of reading, writing, speaking and listening.

The initiative was viewed with interest by the rest of the staff, and it was soon extended to children throughout the school. Parents of

school-age children (particularly those in Year 4) were invited into the school to work with children on basic numeracy and literacy skills. The Learning Support Teacher provided some of the ideas for activities and assessment sheets. The parents who showed an interest in helping in class were offered a place on a six-week training course provided by the Adult Education Service, which gave them information about developing basic skills.

The post of home–school liaison teacher is funded from the school's 'compensatory' budget, which is allocated to schools on the basis of socio-economic factors. Funding to set up the family literacy scheme was secured from the local authority's community fund, which also provided the training course. The LEA subsequently agreed to grant the school £4,000 to extend the initiative. The school used the money to purchase new books for use by parents and to release teachers from their class teaching. The teachers provided some specific training for parent helpers and prepared materials, such as laminated worksheets, which parents use in class.

The strategy

The school has devised a series of activities and projects for parents to work on with their children. Each term, the teachers devise a major activity for their class, such as building a model of a spaceship or a topic requiring written work. There are also whole-school competitions, such as making Easter Bonnets and hanging baskets. The teachers can refer to a folder of ideas, to help them devise games and activities for parents to work on with their children. Each activity is presented with suggestions on how to adapt it according to the needs of the child and a series of 'helpful hints' on how to get the most out of the activity. For example, the 'helpful hints' accompanying a cooking activity include the following advice: *'It's important to let the children do as much as possible for themselves, even if it's not perfect. It doesn't matter if it doesn't turn out quite right. It's the doing that is important. See if the older children can sequence the instructions in the correct order.'*

They are all nice and polite. They help us to learn.

Children are encouraged to bring in the resulting work, which is displayed and used in the classroom.

Portland Primary School
Developing a Partnership for Success

Invaders and Settlers Day

The children will be taking part in an Invaders and Settlers Day on Thursday 10th December. They will have the chance to play games, try food and make things that the Invaders and Settlers would have used.

They will also be able to dress in the type of clothes worn by the Invaders and Settlers. On the back of this letter are three examples of the type of clothes worn by a British warrior, a Roman soldier and a Viking warrior.

Please could you help your child to make a costume to wear on the day. If time and materials are in short supply, a large T-shirt worn with a belt would be an easy alternative.

Thank you for your co-operation.

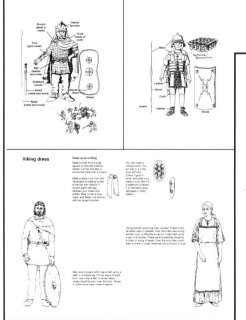

Teacher Planning Sheet				
Jigsaw	Theme/Topic Invaders & Settlers	Area Aware/A4	Date Autumn 98	
Jigsaw Activity	Possible Learning Experiences	National Curriculum Subject Links	Resources (What is sent home)	Evaluation (including number of responses)
To be able to make an Invaders costume to take part in an invaders & settlers day.	To investigate styles of clothing worn. To have first hand experience of dressing in keeping with the period	History English Art Technology	See attached sheet.	Responses 75/80 approx out of 90. Extremely good response and very worthwhile.
				Signed C Amy

During our visit to the school, we observed a session where parents were involved with a group of Year 5 children. The school was holding its literacy period, when children are 'set' according to ability. (This allows an extension group of good readers to be taught in a class of 18 children.)

Five parents were involved in helping ten of the lowest-attaining pupils. At the beginning of the session, the teacher asked the parents to help with children's work towards their individual targets.

Parents assisted with a variety of activities, including encouraging children to complete a whole-class task on phonemes, and a reading comprehension exercise. They also encouraged children to work towards their individual targets. The teacher introduced the whole-class tasks and listened to individual children read. The parents gave prompts and guidance, encouraging children constantly, and helping them to work through the activities at their own pace. The children were quiet and on-task throughout, speaking only to ask parents questions about the activities.

In addition to the activity work, a small group of parents come into the school on three mornings a week. They visit for half an hour at the beginning of the school day. At the time of our visit, each class had about five parents who helped on a regular basis. Most of the parents do not work with their own children.

The school decided to ask parents to support lower-attaining children, because they felt that these children would benefit most from individual attention. Parents work with small groups of two or three children, helping with aspects of their literacy and number work. The children's progress is recorded on a 'jigsaw sheet', which lists a number of different skill areas, each represented on pieces of a jigsaw. Children record their progress by colouring in the relevant piece of the jigsaw when they have completed a task or acquired a skill.

Is it successful?

Most parents have tried out the school's suggestions for activities, and many help their children to enter the school competitions.

One of the major benefits of involving parents in the classroom is that, by providing individual attention, children's attention is focused on their work throughout a session. As one of the teachers pointed out, children have the opportunity to form relationships with adults other than teachers, and parents may have different ways of explaining things which pupils find easier to understand.

The children we spoke to also emphasised the benefits of working with parents. As one boy commented: *'They are all nice and polite. They help us to learn.'* Another child said: *'You can talk things through with them.'* The parents enjoy working with the children, and appreciate the opportunity to build up a relationship with individuals over time. Through working with a small number of children, parents are able to monitor individual progress. As one parent helper said: *'The children receive extra attention. We help to pick up problems that a teacher might not notice.'* Parents also find it interesting to find out about the school's curriculum and teaching

approaches, and are better able to support their own children's learning.

The parents have gained in personal terms: parents who completed the training course received certificates and a volunteer's learning award. Some have gone on to further studies and have gained National Vocational Qualifications as a result.

The children receive extra attention. We help to pick up problems that a teacher might not notice.

The school's 1997 OFSTED inspection report commented on the involvement of parents in children's learning: *'Parents are valued partners. The school has a range of strategies for involving parents in their children's learning in school and at home*,

notably the excellent "Jigsaw" initiative, which benefits pupils through structured homework and targets intensive help to those with greater learning needs.'

Although everyone was in agreement that the initiative had been very successful, the teachers admitted that they had found it difficult to recruit enough new parents to keep it going. Some parents who would like to get involved are unable to do so because they have younger children to look after. The school has recognised this problem and is considering setting up a crèche.

Staff noticed that parents found it difficult to explain some of the concepts to the children that they help. To remedy this, and to ensure consistency in the methods parents use, teachers

now spend the first few sessions of every term demonstrating teaching techniques at the front of the class. The parents are able to copy the teacher until they are confident enough to carry on by themselves.

The school set two success criteria for their initiative. First, they wanted all parents to become fully involved in helping their children to achieve their individual literacy targets. Second, they hoped that the initiative would contribute towards raised standards of literacy throughout the school.

National Curriculum results in literacy have shown a gradual but sustained improvement over recent years, and children's standardised reading test scores have improved relative to their non-verbal test scores. However, owing to the substantial

differences between year-groups and the fact that the school had introduced other strategies to boost reading, the head was reluctant to attribute the improvements to this strategy alone.

What makes it work?

This strategy is an expression of the determination of the head and staff to *'do something about the poor socio-economic situation, rather than just accept it'*. The idea came from one of the teachers, who was able to draw on the support and expertise of the local authority's Community Education Officer and Learning Support Teacher.

The strategy began in the nursery, and parents were encouraged to take part through personal contact with someone from the school during home visits. The school provided an informal environment for parents to learn more about helping their children, and the activities were carefully thought through.

Once the initiative had proved successful with nursery-aged children, the decision was made to expand it. The school is fortunate in having parents who are available during the day and are willing to commit their time to helping other children. Those responsible for planning the initiative recognised that training and materials (such as the 'jigsaw sheets') were key elements in making it work. The school identified clear targets for the initiative, and is monitoring its effectiveness.

Main advantages of this strategy

For pupils

- Through taking part in learning activities with their parents at home, children see that their parents are interested in their progress at school.

- The involvement of parents in the classroom means that pupils receive more individual attention, praise and feedback. As a result, their attention is focused on their work and they are able to progress more rapidly.

- They establish a close working relationship with another adult who is not their teacher.

For teachers and the school as a whole

- The involvement of parents effectively reduces the adult–pupil ratio. Teachers have the opportunity to get an overview of the class and to monitor individual pupils' progress (e.g. it enables teachers to hear children read).

- This initiative ensures that lower-attaining pupils get the extra support and individual attention they need.

- Relationships with parents are strengthened.

- The school's 'jigsaw' initiative has been recognised in their OFSTED inspection report.

For parents

- The school provides parents with clear guidance on how to help their own child at home.

- Parents who visit the school have the satisfaction of helping individual children to make progress in their basic skills. They gain a better understanding of the school's curriculum and teaching methods.

- Some parents have found that their own basic skills have been improved.

- Some parents have attended the authority's training course and have been motivated to attend further training as a result of their involvement in this initiative.

Main disadvantages

- It can be difficult to find sufficient 'new' parents each year to help out in class.

References

BROOKS, G., FLANAGAN, N., HENKHUZENS, Z. and HUTCHISON, D. (1998). *What Works for Slow Readers? The Effectiveness of Early Intervention Schemes.* Slough: NFER.

TOPPING, K. (1995). *Paired Reading, Spelling and Writing: the Handbook for Teachers and Parents.* London: Cassell.

Further reading on involving parents

BASTIANI, J. (1995). *Taking a Few Risks: Learning from Each Other — Teachers, Parents and Pupils.* London: Royal Society for the Encouragement of Arts, Manufactures & Commerce.

TOPPING, K. (1995). *Paired Reading, Spelling and Writing: the Handbook for Teachers and Parents.* London: Cassell.

Video

BASIC SKILLS AGENCY (1998). *Developing Family Literacy: Notes for Teachers* (Four 30 Minute Training Programmes). London: The Basic Skills Agency.

Involving Graduate Volunteers

At St Anne's School, recently graduated young people help out in lessons. They visit the school regularly to work with groups of children on practical activities such as reading, mathematics and science investigations, and art. In some classes, the volunteers work with higher-attaining children and in others, all children take it in turns to work with the volunteers.

Introduction

There have been several recent initiatives to involve adult volunteers in children's education. For example, student mentors have been involved in supporting children's learning outside school hours, and there are a number of well-established business and community mentoring schemes. Supporters of this kind of involvement cite three main areas of potential benefit to pupils: individual attention, advice and interest in children's progress; opportunities to form relationships with adults other than parents and teachers; and the benefits of having positive role models.

About the school

St Anne's is a Catholic primary school with 210 pupils on its roll. It is located in a large council estate on the outskirts of a major city. Although the school draws its children from a variety of backgrounds, a substantial proportion of children come from low-income families (over a third of the children are eligible for free school meals). The school buildings are accessible to wheelchairs and the school accommodates a number of children with physical disabilities. St Anne's has a nursery class and there is one class in each year group from reception to Year 6. Class sizes are relatively small, with none over 30.

The development of the scheme

The school first began to use graduate volunteers in 1996, when a locally based charitable organisation offered to run an after-school club at the school and to organise a play scheme in the summer holidays. The charity is a Christian organisation, which provides opportunities for graduates to work with young people and the local community. Most of the graduates spend a year with the charity immediately following the completion of their degree courses.

After the success of the after-school club, the head approached the charity and asked if the graduates would be prepared to come into the school during the day to help in the classrooms. Initially, graduates were asked to help the 'reluctant readers' in each class. After the first year, the staff noted improvements in these children's reading, and it was decided to expand the scheme to involve the volunteers in helping with other areas of the curriculum.

Security checks are carried out by the charity and all volunteers receive some basic training in working with children before they begin. Once the graduates have indicated which age group they would most like to work with, they are assigned to a particular class teacher. The teacher is then responsible for deciding what they will do in the class and for planning their work.

Is it successful?

Both staff and graduate volunteers feel that the strategy has been successful. They were able to give examples of how individual children had benefited from the additional attention they received from the volunteers. The children we spoke to all had positive things to say about the graduate volunteers. One Year 3 child explained how the volunteer *'makes suggestions about how we can improve our English work'*. A Year 6 child highlighted the importance of the individual attention given by the volunteer: *'I like it because he gives you an individual lesson. You can ask more questions and he gives you suggestions about what we can do.'*

The school runs training sessions for the volunteers at the beginning of each year. These are run by the subject coordinators during the school day, and give the graduates guidance on how to help the children with whom they work.

The strategy

At the time of our visit, six graduates were coming into the school regularly, on one or two days every week. Some of the volunteers have particular areas of expertise that they are keen to share. The head commented: *'We have tended to look at the individuals and tried to make the best of whatever they have had to offer.'* For example, the school arranged for Simon, a physics graduate, to get involved in science lessons.

In the first year of their involvement with the school, the graduates worked on reading with individual children. The volunteers listened to the children read, and helped them with their vocabulary, spelling and word recognition (focusing specifically on the aspects the teacher felt needed to be addressed with each child).

Encouraged by the gains made in reading during the first year, the staff decided to ask the next group of volunteers to target mathematics, as well as helping with other subject areas. This was linked with the school's need to focus on stretching the more able children in mathematics, which was a priority identified in the school development plan. The volunteers are now used to giving support to the more able children in Years 5 and 6, and general assistance to all children in Years 3 and 4.

I like it because he gives you an individual lesson. You can ask more questions and he gives you suggestions about what we can do.

The staff pointed out that the involvement of the volunteers provides the children with good role models. As one teacher said: *'It's nice for the children to know that there is someone from outside who is prepared to give up their time to work with them and I think they respond to that.'* A Year 6 pupil commented: *'It's nice to have other people to ask and to help you out in class, not just the teacher.'*

One teacher suggested that boys (and particularly those from one-parent families) benefited from the opportunity to work with male volunteers. Teachers also commented that the graduates' enthusiasm for their particular subject areas had a positive effect on children's attitudes towards those subjects.

Involvement of the volunteers also effectively reduces the ratio of children to adults. This gives the children opportunities to engage in activities that would not be possible without additional help in the class. The mathematics coordinator said that the involvement of the graduate enabled her to: *'Plan more challenging activities than you can with a class of 35'*, and one of the volunteers commented *'Some of the art stuff I do, the class teacher wouldn't have enough time to do.'* Another volunteer pointed out that because he worked with a group of higher-attaining children, he gave the classteacher an opportunity to focus on needs of the rest of the class.

The only drawback to the graduates' involvement that staff were able to identify was the time commitment involved in liaising with the leader of the charity and providing training sessions for the volunteers.

To determine whether the graduates had influenced the children's reading progress, the teachers administered a standardised reading test immediately before the graduates

became involved, and then repeated the test five months later. The results of the initial tests showed that almost all the 25 selected children had reading ages below their chronological age, in some cases by as much as a year. After working with the volunteers, the children's reading attainment improved by an average of five months in real terms (i.e. in addition to the time that had elapsed between the tests).

It's nice for the children to know that there is someone from outside who is prepared to give up their time to work with them

To evaluate the impact of the graduate volunteers in mathematics, the school is intending to examine results of standardised mathematics tests and National Curriculum results over a three-year period. The head commented that, although there were some gains in relation to National Curriculum results in the first year of the initiative, a more reliable indicator would be to look at trends over a longer period. However, as the school had introduced several initiatives to boost attainment in mathematics, she pointed out that it would be difficult to distinguish the impact of the volunteers' help from that of the other initiatives.

What makes it work?

This school was lucky to have a group of local volunteers to draw on. The charity with which the graduates are based handles the initial selection and security checking. It also ensures that the volunteers have some basic preparation for working with children. The school provides the volunteers with training on how to help children with their school work, and all volunteers are assigned to a teacher who is responsible for liaising with them. As the volunteers visit the school regularly to work with the same group of children, they are able to build up a relationship with the staff and children over a period of a year.

The staff have considered carefully how best to use the additional help provided by the volunteers, and decided to deploy them to help meet the school's development targets, while remaining flexible enough to build on the graduates' own interests and knowledge.

The work of the volunteers is carefully monitored and evaluated. Staff frequently discuss the volunteers' involvement during staff meetings. The school has introduced a 'skills and attitudes' evaluation sheet, which is completed each term by all class teachers responsible for a volunteer. The head signs the sheet and then passes the form to the leader of the charity, who gives feedback to the volunteer. The school has used standardised tests to evaluate the effects of the intervention on children's progress.

Main advantages of this strategy

For pupils

- Children receive more individual attention. They know that someone is interested in them and benefit from immediate help and feedback.

- They are provided with good role models of caring, well-educated young people. The boys from one-parent families, especially, benefit from working with the male volunteers.

- Working with an enthusiastic volunteer may increase the enthusiasm of the children for particular subjects.

- Children who were reluctant to read made good progress with the help of the volunteers.

For staff

- Extra classroom support effectively reduces the ratio of children to adults and allows teachers to concentrate their attention on other groups of children in the class.

- Having another adult in the classroom allows the teacher to introduce more challenging work.

For the school

- The use of graduate volunteers enables the school to work towards its targets for improving children's attainment.

- Children's reading results have improved.

- The charity's involvement has enabled the school to run an after-school club and a summer scheme.

For the volunteers

- Young people are able to spend a year working in the community before moving into employment or further study.

- They develop personal and social skills and learn how to communicate with children.

- The volunteers build up positive, rewarding relationships with children and teachers.

Main disadvantages

- No real disadvantages to the school were identified, apart from the time taken in liaising with the charity and providing training for the graduates at the beginning of each academic year.

Further reading on involving volunteers

BALL, M. (1998). *Community Partnerships: Practical Guidelines for Involving Volunteers in Study Support Centres.* London: The Prince's Trust.

DANIEL, A. (Ed) (1995). *Learning Together: the Added Value of Student Tutors Volunteering in Schools.* London: Community Service Volunteers.

EDUCATION EXTRA (1998). *Schools and Volunteers: a Good Practice Guide to Using Volunteers After School.* London: Education Extra.

An After-School Homework Club

Over recent years, Silverleigh Primary School has introduced many different initiatives aimed at raising pupil achievement. These include: taking part in the pilot phase of the National Literacy Strategy; a new approach to teaching mathematics; measures to improve attendance; and a new behaviour policy. For the purposes of this report, we decided to focus on just one of the school's strategies: their after-school homework club.

Introduction

The Government has published guidelines endorsing the importance of homework in helping children to make progress at school (GB. DfEE. SEU, 1998). The DfEE recommends that all primary schools have a policy for homework and should set homework regularly, ranging from an hour a week in Years 1 and 2 to 30 minutes a day for Years 5 and 6.

Children need a quiet environment in which to study, but this is not always available in the home. The Government is committed to an expansion of study support facilities for children, and has set a target for half of all secondary schools and a quarter of all primaries to offer children opportunities to study outside school hours by the year 2001. The expansion will be supported by funding from the National Lottery New Opportunities Fund (GB. DfEE, 1998).

About the school

Silverleigh Primary School is an inner-city school with 140 children on its roll. It is situated in a deprived area: over 40 per cent of the local men are unemployed and 88 per cent of the school's pupils are entitled to free school meals. There is a high crime rate in the local area. Five children have statements of special educational need and 52 are on the special needs register.

The school has six classes, from reception to Year 6, and there are six full-time teachers in addition to the head. A part-time auxiliary works with the children with special educational needs and two other part-time members of staff help with work on numeracy and literacy.

The development of the strategy

The head was keen to develop a homework strategy as part of the school's central commitment to raising standards in mathematics and English. Staff devised a homework policy, which emphasised the importance of homework in developing children's independent learning skills, enabling children to extend their skills, knowledge and interests, and involving parents and other family members in children's learning. The policy stated that homework should be set for all pupils on a regular basis each week, and the school introduced 'Homework Planners' (booklets for children to record their homework assignments).

The idea of a homework club came about because teachers were becoming frustrated by children's apparent reluctance to complete their homework. When they investigated the reasons for this, they found that many children lacked a quiet place at home to complete their work, or

did not have access to basic materials such as pens, paper and books.

The homework club was established in 1996. The school sent letters to all parents, asking whether they thought their child might attend, and about a third expressed an interest. The staff then decided which was the best night of the week for them, and drew up a simple set of guidelines. Teachers volunteered to give their time to staff the club. The school sent another letter to parents announcing that the club would be free of charge and open to all children, provided that the parents gave written permission. In order to address the school's concerns about children's safety, parents were asked to state who would be collecting their child from the homework club. The letter made it clear that children who volunteered to attend the club would be expected to attend on a regular basis.

It's less boring than home, less boring than watching TV. I like everything about it.

Having attempted to raise money for the club from a variety of sources, the head was eventually able to secure about £350 from local businesses. This was spent on basic supplies, such as pens, stationery and crates to store materials. There were also some

donations 'in kind': a local hotel donated some unwanted cardboard folders and computer equipment was given by three other businesses. Some of this support was generated after the club was set up, when an article about it appeared in the local newspaper.

The strategy

The homework club takes place after school on Tuesday evenings and the session lasts about an hour. The class teachers assemble the children and take a crate of materials with them to the school hall. The children sit in their year groups around clusters of tables. Each teacher works with the children from their own class, offering help with particular difficulties, and helping children to develop independent learning skills. Children work alone, in pairs or as a group, depending on the task at hand.

Children have access to resources such as pens, paper and reference books, and some are able to use one of the school's computers. The staff provide all children with a drink and a snack. Children who attend the club regularly are rewarded with a

certificate signed and presented by the headteacher.

Is it successful?

The main successes of the homework club have been its popularity among children, the opportunities provided for teachers and children to get to know one another better and the contribution of the club to children's learning.

When the homework club first started, the head suggested to the staff that if 15 per cent of the children attended on a regular basis, they should consider it a success. However, recruitment has far exceeded this target and the club has consistently attracted about half of the school's population.

The staff, pupils and parents we spoke to all talked about the children's enthusiasm for the club. One parent described her children's reactions as follows: *'Every week they want to know "When is it homework club, when is it homework club?". They would have it every day if they could. They're really mad on it, they think it's very exciting, it is the best thing.'* Similarly, a Year 6 child said: *'It's less boring than home, less boring than watching TV. I like everything about it.'*

The head felt that the children's enthusiasm for the club has had a positive effect on staff morale. The club has demonstrated that children are willing and eager to learn, and are prepared to devote time to homework.

Silverleigh Homework Club Guidelines

1   The club will meet each Tuesday after school and will operate from 3.15 pm to 4.15 pm in the school Hall.

2   Attendance at the Homework Club will be free and will be available to all of our pupils from reception – Year 6, subject to the class teacher having received the appropriate written permission from each child's parent(s) for the child to attend.

3   No child will be prevented from attending the Homework Club unless their behaviour is such that the Headteacher and staff consider it likely to disrupt the learning of other pupils. In such circumstances the Headteacher will inform parents that their child will not be allowed to attend the Homework Club for a specified period of time.

4   Parents will be informed, in writing, of their responsibility to make appropriate, safe arrangements for their children to go home at the end of each session of the Homework Club.

5   Homework must be set by each child's class teacher.

6   All teaching staff have opted to participate in supervising Homework Club sessions and arrangements have been made on that basis. Consequently staff are expected to maintain this regular commitment. (Variation can only be by prior arrangement with the Headteacher).

7   Staff are responsible for setting out and tidying away equipment.

8   Staff should encourage parents and other helpers (known to teachers/Headteacher) to help with Homework Club on a regular basis.

9   In the event of Homework Club having to be cancelled all parents will be given the maximum amount of notice possible (not less than 24 hours – except in an emergency).

10 All efforts must be made to make attendance at Homework Club as pleasant an experience as possible.

The fact that attendance at the club is voluntary for both teachers and pupils means that there is a different, more informal atmosphere than during lessons. As one of the teachers commented: *'Children are meeting staff in a slightly different context. Because it's after school, they see teachers in a very friendly capacity.'* The head suggested that teachers also learned more about the children who attended the club: *'I think our perceptions of the children have been extended considerably through this. You see children in a different context, and sometimes we've been pleasantly surprised, for instance with some of the older ones, how supportive they've been of the younger children.'*

There was also evidence that the club has contributed to improved relationships between parents and staff. Some parents have become involved in helping at the club and many have expressed their appreciation to teachers for giving their time for this purpose. When parents come to collect their children, there are opportunities for them to speak to teachers about their child's progress. The parents' positive reaction has demonstrated to teachers that they support the school and are interested in their children's progress at school.

Everyone we spoke to said they felt that the club had had a major impact on the children's learning. The head said: *'It contributes to a learning culture in the school. Standards of literacy and numeracy have definitely improved through the homework club. I think there is a fairly strong correlation between the progress the children are making and their attendance at homework club.'*

About six months after the club began, the head asked parents and children to complete a short questionnaire about the club. A high proportion responded. Replies from both parents and children indicated that the club had helped to improve children's learning and confidence. Parents commented that the club provided their children with an appropriate environment in which to complete their homework, which some acknowledged was not available at home. The questionnaire invited parents and pupils to suggest ways in which the club could be improved. The only suggestion for improvement was that the school should run the club more often.

The teachers are prepared to give up their time to staff the club because they are convinced of its benefits. Ideally, the head would have liked to raise sufficient funds to bring in some additional staff to run the club, but this has proved impossible. The head commented that the organisation and administration required to set up the club were fairly demanding but pointed out that these became much easier once the club was up and running. However, there is the continuing need to find new sources of funding in order to cover the club's running costs.

What makes it work?

This school has introduced a number of different strategies, all of which are designed to promote raising standards in mathematics and English. The staff are committed to this goal, and the head tries to ensure that each new initiative has time to become established before staff turn their attention to the next.

Teachers recognised that homework could make an important contribution to raising standards and developing children's study skills. In order to address the problem of poor homework completion, teachers drew up a homework policy to be adopted throughout the school. Before going ahead with the idea of establishing an after-school club, the school contacted all parents to check on the level of support for the idea. The head recognised that the initiative would require some additional funding, and was able to generate some business sponsorship and donations of equipment.

It contributes to a learning culture in the school. Standards of literacy and numeracy have definitely improved through the homework club.

All staff have supported the initiative. They drew up some simple rules to ensure children's safety and to encourage their commitment to the club. Once established, the club was relatively easy to run. The school made sure that they had procedures in place for monitoring the effect of the club. They set an initial target for participation, monitored attendance and checked that it was achieving its goals by asking pupils and parents to complete a short questionnaire.

Main advantages of this strategy

For pupils

- The homework club provides children with an opportunity to complete their homework in a quiet and supportive atmosphere. This is particularly beneficial for children who lack a suitable space for quiet study at home.

- Children enjoy taking part. The club represents a popular alternative to spending time watching TV or doing homework on their own at home.

- The club provides children with the opportunity to meet staff in a less formal context, which has increased their confidence in talking to teachers.

- Because older and younger children work alongside each other, there are opportunities to work collaboratively and to develop social skills.

- The club enables children to receive additional help in those areas where they most need it.

For teachers

- The club ensures that all children have the opportunity to complete their homework on time.

- The club enables staff to see the children in a different, more positive context.

- Staff have an additional opportunity to liaise with parents.

- The positive reaction to the homework club from children and parents has boosted teachers' morale.

For parents

- The homework club provides facilities and support for children, which many parents are unable to provide at home.

- Parents can get more involved with the school through helping out at the homework club.

- Parents have informal opportunities to speak to teachers about their child's progress when collecting their children from the club.

For the school

- The homework club helps children to develop a culture of learning.

- The club is one of a number of initiatives that have contributed to raising standards of numeracy and literacy throughout the school.

- The club has helped the school to establish good relationships with parents.

- As a result of this initiative, the school received positive coverage in the local newspaper.

Main disadvantages

- All teachers have to give up an hour of their own time each week to staff the club. The school does not have the means to pay staff for their extra work.

- There are ongoing costs which cannot be met through school funds, so the school must devote time to fundraising in order to cover running costs. The lack of funding places constraints on the school's ability to expand its after-school provision.

References

GREAT BRITAIN. DEPARTMENT FOR EDUCATION AND EMPLOYMENT (1998). *Extending Opportunity: a National Framework for Study Support.* London: DfEE.

GREAT BRITAIN. DEPARTMENT FOR EDUCATION AND EMPLOYMENT. STANDARDS AND EFFECTIVENESS UNIT (1998). *Homework: Guidelines for Primary and Secondary Schools.* London: DfEE.

Further reading on study support and homework

EDUCATION EXTRA (1998). *Succeeding at Study Support: an Evaluation of 12 Model Projects in Primary and Secondary Schools.* London: Education Extra.

GREAT BRITAIN. DEPARTMENT FOR EDUCATION AND EMPLOYMENT. STANDARDS AND EFFECTIVENESS UNIT (1998). *Homework: Guidelines for Primary and Secondary Schools.* London: DfEE.

WESTON, P. (1999). *Homework: Learning from Practice.* London: The Stationery Office.

Resources

DEVISING STRATEGIES TO RAISE ACHIEVEMENT: A PLANNING GUIDE

The purpose of this guide is to build on and supplement the work that schools are already doing as part of their process of self-review. The guide is designed to help heads, governors and teachers to identify and plan an appropriate strategy for raising achievement at KS2. It could be completed individually, or used as a basis for group decision-making.

1. Diagnosing problem areas

This part of the process is designed to help you to identify which areas of teaching and learning are most in need of development.

1.1 Which areas of pupils' achievement do you consider to be most in need of improvement? Check for evidence of underachievement in:

- Key Stage 2 assessment results (in relation to national and local targets);
- 'value added' between KS1 and KS2;
- other test results (e.g. standardised reading or mathematics tests);
- OFSTED inspection report;
- portfolios of children's work;
- classroom observation (e.g. as part of appraisal);
- teachers' perceptions;
- other sources (e.g. school, class or individual targets).

1.2 Which areas of the basic curriculum are most in need of attention?

❏ Mathematics ❏ English
❏ Science ❏ Design and technology
❏ Information technology ❏ Music
❏ Art ❏ PE
❏ Geography ❏ History
❏ RE

1.3 Which specific aspect(s) of the subject areas need most attention (e.g. speaking and listening)?

1.4 Is there a need to tackle any of the following underlying causes of underachievement?

❑ Gender differences

❑ Underperformance of children from different ethnic backgrounds

❑ Underperformance by children within a particular ability band

❑ Underperformance of children in a specific age-group

❑ Poor attendance

❑ Disruptive behaviour

❑ Poor social/interpersonal skills

❑ Lack of study skills

❑ Low self-esteem

❑ Lack of motivation

❑ Social deprivation *(e.g. lack of educational resources in the home)*

❑ Other issues *(please add)*

1.5 Having considered the evidence, you may find it helpful to write a short statement about the area of underachievement that you feel most needs to be tackled.

2. Choosing a strategy

This part of the process aims to help you choose the type of intervention that will enhance the climate for learning and raise your pupils' achievement. We have adapted an existing framework of strategies (Weindling, 1999) to reflect the range of strategies identified in this research.

Look at the types of strategy and accompanying examples: which do you feel would be most suitable for use in your school? *Your strategy could take elements from two or more of the categories outlined opposite, but it may be best to restrict your efforts to one or two strategies at any one time.*

Additional support

Additional help and individual attention is provided for children. The support may come from adults or children, from within or outside the school.

- Individual reading support/peer tutoring schemes.
- Redeployment of staff to offer more intensive support to particular pupils.
- Parental involvement in supporting children's learning at home or in school.
- Mentors and other volunteers.
- Artists-in-schools schemes.

Specialist teaching

Employing teachers with subject knowledge/expertise to teach specific areas of the curriculum.

- Members of staff are responsible for teaching a particular area of the curriculum to pupils from more than one class.
- Teachers with specialist knowledge act as mentors and provide training for other staff.
- The school buys in additional specialist help from agencies or employs part-time specialist staff.

New teaching methods and resources

Initiatives involving changing teaching and learning, intensive intervention programmes and additional educational resources.

- New initiatives to develop social, behavioural, or intellectual skills.
- Purchase of new educational resources (e.g. computers, books).

Ability grouping

Strategies may be aimed at improving the achievement of groups of pupils by differentiating teaching and learning in relation to pupils' ability or attainment.

- Within-class grouping and setting.
- Initiatives targeted on children in specific ability bands (e.g. withdrawal from class of pupils who are not achieving up to their potential).

Increasing learning time

This includes strategies to increase time on specific areas of the curriculum, or increasing the total time available for learning within the school day.

- Providing more time for particular areas of the curriculum.
- Restructuring the school day to provide more learning time.

Study support and homework

This includes specific policies, support and facilities for homework and other learning activities taking place outside of school hours (before school, during the lunchtime break, after school, at weekends and during the school holidays).

- Implementing a policy on homework, including home reading schemes.
- Providing support for 'curriculum extension' at school (e.g. a study centre or homework club).
- Providing study support for 'enrichment' activities (e.g. clubs, sports and arts activities).

Target setting

This involves pupils in the process of target setting and monitoring individual progress to improve achievement in academic, personal and/or social terms.

- Target setting for groups of pupils.
- Involving pupils in individual target setting.

Other strategies

- E.g. improved curriculum planning.

2.1 Having looked at the list of strategies, which type of intervention(s) do you think would help you to meet your pupils' needs?

2.2 Do you need more information and advice before you can make a final decision? You could:

- look at some of the case-study examples and see whether you think a similar strategy would be useful in your school;

- follow up some of the further reading and contact organisations listed in the back of this book;

- find out what is going on in your area (e.g. through your link adviser, or by using your own networks);

- arrange for staff to visit a school which has tried an interesting initiative.

When you are in a position to select your strategy, and are sure that it is the right one for your school, please move onto the next part of this guide.

3. Putting it into practice

3.1 What is the main aim of your intervention?

Success criteria

Success criteria are short statements setting targets for your chosen initiative. They are useful in ensuring that everyone has a clear idea of what the initiative is trying to achieve and in monitoring progress and evaluating the impact of the strategy. When setting success criteria, try to make them specific, measurable, achievable/realistic and time-limited (see GB. DfEE and OFSTED, 1996)

3.2 The success criteria for this initiative are:

3.3 Who will be responsible for overseeing the strategy (i.e. the coordinator)?

3.4 Who else will be involved in overseeing it? *(Would it be useful to involve other members of staff or parents, governors, pupils, in managing the strategy?)*

Resources

Depending on the scope of the initiative, you may wish to draw up a budget and seek additional funding.

3.5 Which resources will you need?

- Staff time (who will be involved and how much of their time will be required)?
- In-service training.
- Cover to release teachers for planning/training.
- Equipment and materials.
- Evaluation costs (e.g. purchase of assessment materials).

3.6 Where could you obtain the funding?

- Internal sources (e.g. existing curriculum and INSET budgets).
- Fundraising.
- LEA.
- National Lottery.
- Commercial/business sponsorship.
- Other sources.

Timing

It may help to draw up a rough timetable, taking account of the following points.

- When would be a good time to begin?
- What preparations need to take place beforehand?
- How long do you want the initiative to last?
- Will you need to hold planning meetings (if so, at what stages during the initiative)?
- When will you need to assess and report on progress (e.g. at certain staff meetings, do you need to compile a report for the project's sponsor)?

Monitoring and evaluation

How will you monitor the progress of the initiative (to make sure things are going as planned)? How will you know whether your initiative has had the desired effect on the children? How will you document unexpected consequences?

The kind of information you need to collect will relate to the success criteria you have identified. Some suggestions are listed below:

- assessment results (e.g. results from standardised tests);
- quality of children's work (e.g. from examining examples of work produced by pupils of different levels of ability);
- attendance/participation rates (e.g. for voluntary activities);
- participants' views (e.g. a questionnaire survey);
- noting reactions to the initiative from children, parents and staff.

3.7 The methods we will use to monitor and evaluate our initiative are:

Informing others

It is worth considering how best to inform others about the new initiative. This includes not only those members of staff directly involved, but others, such as governors, pupils and parents. At a later stage, you may wish to seek publicity for your initiative (e.g. by holding an event to celebrate success to which you can invite parents/local press).

3.8 We will inform   by these methods

- ❏ Staff
- ❏ Parents
- ❏ Governors
- ❏ Pupils

Reference

WEINDLING, D. (1999). 'Kissing the frog: moving from school effectiveness to school improvement', *TOPIC*, Issue 21, Item 2.

Further reading on target setting

CLARKE, S. (1998). *Targeting Assessment in the Primary Classroom: Strategies for Planning, Assessment, Pupil Feedback and Target Setting.* London: Hodder & Stoughton.

GREAT BRITAIN. DEPARTMENT FOR EDUCATION AND EMPLOYMENT and OFFICE FOR STANDARDS IN EDUCATION (1996). *Setting Targets to Raise Standards: a Survey of Good Practice* (Improving Schools Series). London: DfEE.

Further Reading

The books suggested as further reading are described here. We have divided them into a number of thematic sections, which reflect the issues addressed in the case studies. The books are listed in alphabetical order by author within each section.

Information technology

CROMPTON, R. and MANN, P. (Eds) (1996). *IT Across the Primary Curriculum*. London: Cassell.
This book explores the potential uses of information technology in primary teaching. It begins with an introduction to the current educational climate and the IT programmes of study. The following chapters address the areas within the programmes of study and provide examples on: communicating information through words, art and music; handling information; computer modelling, control and organisation. The book also deals with issues of assessment, policy and staff development. It is illustrated throughout with cartoons, photographs, and examples of children's work.

HARRISON, M. (1998). *Coordinating Information and Communications Technology Across the Primary School*. London: Falmer Press.
Designed as a subject leader's handbook, this book provides comprehensive coverage of information and communications technology. It is divided into five main sections, dealing with: the role of the IT coordinator; what IT coordinators need to know; developing policy; monitoring and evaluation; and resources for learning (useful addresses for information and supplies).

SCHOOL CURRICULUM AND ASSESSMENT AUTHORITY (1997). *Expectations in Information Technology at Key Stages 1 and 2*. London: SCAA.
This booklet is intended to be of practical help to subject coordinators and teachers in planning, teaching and assessing children's progress in IT. The first section sets out expectations for children's achievements by the end of Years 2, 4 and 6. The second section provides examples of children's work, which are accompanied by an explanation of the context in which the work was planned and how it relates to the IT programmes of study.

Mathematics and numeracy

NATIONAL NUMERACY PROJECT (1998). *Numeracy Lessons*. London: BEAM.
This practical book describes a series of lessons on number designed for each year group from reception to Year 7. The book is designed to be used within the framework set out for the National Numeracy Project.

FIELKER, D. (1993). *Starting from Your Head: Mental Geometry*. London: BEAM.
FIELKER, D. (1993). *Starting from Your Head: Mental Number*. London: BEAM.
These two booklets set out a series of activities that teachers can use to teach mental mathematics to children in Key stages 2 and 3.

SCHOOL CURRICULUM AND ASSESSMENT AUTHORITY (1997). *Mathematics and the Use of Language: Key Stages 1 & 2*. London: SCAA.
This leaflet considers the relationship between mathematics and language skills. It poses two key questions: in what ways can work in mathematics help to develop speaking, listening, writing and reading skills; and how can children's understanding of mathematics be enhanced by developing these skills? The leaflet illustrates the links between mathematics and language skills and provides examples of how these can be enhanced through mathematics teaching. There is also a section on longer-term planning for language skill development in mathematics.

Literacy

BROOKS, G., FLANAGAN, N., HENKHUZENS, Z. and HUTCHISON, D. (1998). *What Works for Slow Readers? The Effectiveness of Early Intervention Schemes*. Slough: NFER.
Teachers wishing to support slow readers have numerous schemes and methods to choose from. This report reviews about 30 reading intervention schemes in use in this country, describes their key characteristics and considers the evidence on their effectiveness. The book also highlights common characteristics of successful strategies for helping children's reading development.

TOPPING, K. (1995). *Paired Reading, Spelling and Writing: the Handbook for Teachers and Parents.* London: Cassell.

This book is a 'how to' guide for teachers interested in using paired approaches to develop children's literacy skills. The author presents the evidence on the effectiveness of paired approaches and offers practical guidance to help teachers to organise and evaluate their own schemes. The book includes a set of 'reproducibles' (photocopiable sheets, checklists and certificates for use in paired literacy schemes).

Raising boys' achievement

ARNOT, M., GRAY, J., JAMES, M. and RUDDUCK, J. with DUVEEN, G. (1998). *Recent Research on Gender and Educational Performance* (OFSTED Reviews of Research). London: The Stationery Office.

The aim of this review is to extend enquiry and debate on the subject of gender and educational performance. It provides a summary of resent research in the area, including sections on: the size and nature of the gender gap; educational and social explanations; and the effects of single-sex schools. The final chapter focuses on school strategies for addressing gender inequality, such as single-sex grouping, role modelling, data analysis and mentoring. The authors conclude that gender gaps in educational performance are a national problem. However, there are no simple explanations for gender differences in performance, and several factors are likely to have an influence in any given context.

BLEACH, K. (Ed) (1998). *Raising Boys' Achievement in Schools.* Stoke-on-Trent: Trentham Books.

The subject of boys' underachievement has been the cause of much comment and speculation. This book aims to provide a better understanding of the problem and to offer some practical solutions. It begins with an introductory chapter on the factors responsible for underachievement and poor behaviour among boys. This is followed by a series of chapters providing examples of how schools and LEAs have tackled the issue. In one of the chapters, Colin Noble describes the measures adopted in Kirklees primary schools to help boys do better. Their strategies included 'shared reading', in which Year 6 boys supported boys in Year 3.

MacDONALD, A., SAUNDERS, L. and BENEFIELD, P. (1999). *Boys' Achievement, Progress, Motivation and Participation: Issues Raised by the Recent Literature.* Slough: NFER.

This report reviews the recent literature on the subject of boys' achievement. It considers the evidence for some of the commonly-held views about the causes of boys' underachievement at school and discusses the complex inter-relationships between achievement and gender, social class and ethnicity. The authors conclude that literacy and language play a key role in raising boys' achievement. They emphasise the role of teachers in encouraging all pupils to develop positive attitudes towards learning; and in influencing boys' willingness to read and choice of reading material in particular.

QUALIFICATIONS AND CURRICULUM AUTHORITY (1998). *Can Do Better: Raising Boys' Achievement in English.* London: QCA.

In response to boys' relatively poor performance in English, this book aims to provoke thought and put forward ideas for action. It provides a breakdown of the National Curriculum requirements in English and makes suggestions to help teachers engage the interest of boys. There is a chapter on how to research the issue in schools (for example, through examining pupils' work or interviewing pupils). The book provides a series of suggestions for action and is illustrated with case-study examples.

PICKERING, J. (1997). *Raising Boys' Achievement* (School Effectiveness Series). Stafford: Network Educational Press.

This book draws on both school-based research and examples of good practice. It is divided into three parts. Part One contains activities to help teachers consider the evidence on patterns of boys' achievement at their school. Part Two presents commonly held views and evidence about the causes of boys' underachievement and suggested solutions. It includes a series of case studies looking at specific aspects of boys' underachievement. Part Three invites readers to reflect on what they have discovered. The book's features include advanced organisers, 'stimulus quotations', and checklists. It contains a set of recommended reading and contact addresses.

Addressing the needs of children from ethnic minorities

GILLBORN, D. and GIPPS, C. (1996). *Recent Research on the Achievements of Ethnic Minority Pupils* (OFSTED Reviews of Research). London: HMSO.

This is a review of research evidence on the achievement of ethnic minority pupils in England, following the publication of the 'Swann Report' in 1985. The review reveals differential patterns of achievement and progress among pupils from specific ethnic minority groups, and in relation to gender and social class. It points to the important influence of ethnic background and fluency in English on performance at primary level. The authors conclude that, while there have been encouraging developments in the past decade, there is a continued need to monitor the achievements and needs of pupils from different ethnic groups. They suggest that schools should strive to raise standards for all pupils, while introducing whole-school policies to address ethnic diversity and reduce racial harassment.

OFFICE FOR STANDARDS IN EDUCATION (1999). *Raising the Attainment of Minority Ethnic Pupils: School and LEA Responses*. London: OFSTED.

Following on from the review reported above, this report is the result of an inspection of initiatives aimed to raise the attainment of children from minority ethnic groups. It is based on discussions with officers in 25 LEAs and visits to 34 schools identified as demonstrating elements of good practice. The authors draw attention to patterns of underachievement among certain minority ethnic groups and describe the initiatives adopted by LEAs and schools to improve provision and raise attainment. The report contains a series of recommendations for schools and LEAs, including the need for effective monitoring of pupil achievement and behaviour by ethnic group, and for the development of school policy to address key issues.

Addressing the needs of higher-attaining children

EYRE, D. (1997). *Able Children in Ordinary Schools*. London: David Fulton.

Deborah Eyre is President of the National Association for Able and Gifted Children in Education. In this book, she aims to help schools to address the needs of their most able pupils. The book considers issues of defining and identifying able children and outlines a differentiated approach to classroom planning and provision. There is a chapter on issues in primary schools, which deals with practical concerns, such as: staff responsibilities and the role of the coordinator; staff development; school provision for enrichment and extension; and withdrawal activities. There is guidance on writing a school policy for able children, and a bibliography of books on the subject.

FREEMAN, J. (1998). *Educating the Very Able: Current International Research* (OFSTED Reviews of Research). London: The Stationery Office.

This review summarises international research into able children and provides summary points on practical issues, such as: how to identify able children (including those from disadvantaged backgrounds); how to recognise signs of underachievement; the effects of educational acceleration; curriculum organisation; teaching approaches; and policy development.

TEARE, B. (1997). *Effective Provision for Able & Talented Children*. Stafford: Network Educational Press.

This book in the 'School Effectiveness Series' focuses on practical ideas for teachers. It explains why schools should make provision for able and talented children and goes on to outline a policy for meeting the needs of these children in school. Guidance is provided on: identifying able and talented children; school ethos; staffing; and the coordinator's role. The book puts forward a range of strategies for improving provision in the classroom, including a section on monitoring and evaluation. There is an extensive list of resources and further reading.

Cooperative learning and group development

BLISS, T., ROBINSON, G. and MAINES, B. (1998). *Developing Circle Time*. London: Lucky Duck Publishing.

Circle Time provides opportunities for children to enhance their self-esteem. This booklet aims to support teachers to help all children achieve their potential. The theory behind Circle Time is described, along with the developmental stages that members of the group experience. There is a detailed section on getting started, which provides examples of a term's work. The appendix contains numerous worksheets that can be used in Circle Time sessions. The authors have also produced a video entitled *Coming Round to Circle Time*, which provides examples of activities used for different purposes. The video is available from the same publishers.

DUNNE, E. and BENNETT, N. (1990). *Talking and Learning in Groups: Activity Based In-service and Pre-service Materials* (Leverhulme Primary Project Classroom Skills Series). Basingstoke: Macmillan Education.

Based on the researchers' experiences during the Leverhulme Primary Project, this book aims to provide practical guidance and discussion materials for teachers interested in using cooperative groupwork techniques in the classroom. It is divided into six units, which cover: the research and theoretical context; different forms of grouping; choice of groups; management and training; monitoring and assessment; and guidance on setting up groupwork in the classroom. The book contains numerous activities designed to provoke discussion, written response and practical application.

Discipline and behaviour

DOCKING, J. (1996). *Managing Behaviour in the Primary School*. 2nd edn. London: David Fulton.

Written in response to the Elton Report on discipline in schools, this book provides advice on effective behaviour management, including how to pre-empt problems, reinforce and develop good behaviour and respond to poor behaviour. There is advice on developing a whole-school policy, managing behaviour in the playground and combating bullying. The book is aimed at experienced staff as well as students and newly qualified teachers. It includes checklists, examples and a list of recommended reading.

WATKINS, C. (1997). *Managing Classroom Behaviour: a Bit Like Air Traffic Control*. London: Association of Teachers and Lecturers.

The ATL commissioned this guidance in response to concerns about school behaviour and a perceived lack of support and training for teachers on classroom management. The short report presents scenarios of common classroom situations, explains some of the basic principles of encouraging positive behaviour and poses questions to help teachers to examine their own practice.

Setting and ability grouping

HARLEN, W. and MALCOLM, H. (1997). *Setting and Streaming: a Review of Research* (Using Research Series 18). Edinburgh: SCRE.

This book reviews the 'best evidence' from research into the effects of grouping pupils by ability. It outlines the use and effects of streaming, setting and within-class grouping, emphasising the relationship between particular types of grouping and their use in different subject areas. The book concludes that ability grouping has no overall effect on pupil achievement within primary schools. However, evidence revealed that pupils of all abilities benefit from within-class ability grouping in mathematics.

OFFICE FOR STANDARDS IN EDUCATION (1998). *Setting in Primary Schools*. London: OFSTED.

In 1997/98, OFSTED carried out an investigation into the use of setting by ability in English primary schools. This report is based on evidence from OFSTED school inspections, together with surveys and visits to schools. The report notes that setting is becoming increasingly popular, and is most often used for teaching mathematics and English in Years 5 and 6. The report discusses the evidence for an association between the introduction of setting and raising standards. It goes on to outline aspects of good practice in managing the implementation of setting and discusses implications for the curriculum and teaching.

SUKHNANDAN, L. with LEE, B. (1998). *Streaming, Setting and Grouping by Ability: a Review of the Literature*. Slough: NFER.

This report highlights research findings on streaming, setting and within-class grouping. It concludes that results have been somewhat inconsistent, but there is a general finding that setting and streaming have no significant effects, either positive or negative, on overall pupil achievement. However, several studies have identified negative outcomes of setting and streaming, such as detrimental effects on the attitudes and self-esteem of middle- and lower-ability children, and the reinforcement of existing social divisions (in terms of social class, race, gender and season of birth). The report concludes that schools should assess their own needs in relation to the organisation of teaching groups and should monitor their systems carefully to address any possible negative effects of grouping children by ability.

Subject specialist teaching

OFFICE FOR STANDARDS IN EDUCATION (1997). *Using Subject Specialism to Promote High Standards at Key Stage 2: an Illustrative Survey.* London: OFSTED.

In order to investigate the contribution of subject specialism to the quality of teaching and improving standards, OFSTED carried out a survey of 70 schools. The inspection visits involved interviews, observations of lessons and a review of documents (such as policies, guidelines and schemes of work). The report presents findings from the inspectors' visits and includes seven case studies illustrating some of the ways in which primary schools can introduce subject specialism.

Transition between primary and secondary school

QUALIFICATIONS AND CURRICULUM AUTHORITY (1998). *Building Bridges: Guidance and Training Materials for Teachers of Year 6 and Year 7 Pupils.* London: QCA.

The authors of this booklet state that there is 'considerable evidence' that pupils do not make the progress they should in the early part of Key Stage 3. The booklet aims to help schools to improve the analysis, dissemination and use of information passed from primary to secondary schools. It recommends a number of strategies to aid transfer, such as using a common transfer form and holding joint planning meetings for primary and secondary school staff. The booklet outlines suggested INSET activities and contains a set of sample documents.

Target setting

CLARKE, S. (1998). *Targeting Assessment in the Primary Classroom: Strategies for Planning, Assessment, Pupil Feedback and Target Setting.* London: Hodder & Stoughton.

This practical book begins with a statement of the purposes, principles and definitions of assessment and

provides guidance on structuring an assessment policy. Chapters deal with issues such as: curriculum planning; sharing learning intentions and involving pupils; target setting at school, class and pupil level; and celebrating achievement. It ends with a commentary on current assessment approaches. The text is illustrated throughout with quotes from Government reports, samples of plans and children's work.

GREAT BRITAIN. DEPARTMENT FOR EDUCATION AND EMPLOYMENT and OFFICE FOR STANDARDS IN EDUCATION (1996). *Setting Targets to Raise Standards: a Survey of Good Practice* (Improving Schools Series). London: DfEE.

The Secretary of State for Education asked the DfEE and OFSTED to look at schools' existing practice in order to help schools develop effective target-setting strategies as part of the drive to meet the National Targets for Education and Training. This short report covers issues of school leadership, use of performance data, raising parents' expectations and the role of external review and support. The book contains numerous examples of schools' target-setting practice, together with action points and planning guides.

Involving parents and volunteers

BALL, M. (1998). *Community Partnerships: Practical Guidelines for Involving Volunteers in Study Support Centres.* London: The Prince's Trust.

This book considers the use of volunteers in study support for young people. It begins by defining study support and its place within the community, and looks in detail at the role of business mentors and student teacher/mentors. The main part of the book is taken up with a practical guide aiming to help readers to 'get the best out of volunteers'. This covers such issues as project design and management, recruitment and screening volunteers, induction and training, costs and review. The book contains a list of agencies/networks and sample documents (such as a model policy for volunteers and a sample questionnaire for mentors).

BASIC SKILLS AGENCY (1998). *Developing Family Literacy* (Four 30-Minute Training Programmes) [Video]. London: Basic Skills Agency.

The Basic Skills Agency produced this 30-minute video to show teachers some approaches to working with parents and children. It argues that, while many of the approaches to working with children will be familiar to teachers, the distinctive features of family literacy are the context and the combined work with parents and children. The video explains some of the approaches to developing early literacy skills and shows examples of schemes based in primary schools.

BASTIANI, J. (1995). *Taking a Few Risks: Learning from Each Other — Teachers, Parents and Pupils.* London: Royal Society for the Encouragement of Arts, Manufacturers & Commerce.

This book draws together the experiences of parents, pupils and teachers working together to improve the quality of children's learning experiences. It is based on a two-year research project aimed at promoting the benefits of partnerships between parents and schools. The book describes the experience of ten primary and secondary schools and draws together some of the common themes to offer guidance on policy and practice.

DANIEL, A. (Ed) (1995). *Learning Together: the Added Value of Student Tutors Volunteering in Schools.* London: Community Service Volunteers.

This book comprises a series of articles by different authors, who each describe their experiences of schemes using student volunteers. The book is divided into eight sections, dealing with a variety of issues such as: the role of student tutors in schools; quality assurance; and the roles of the various partners and stakeholders. The book provides references, contact addresses and lists of resources.

EDUCATION EXTRA (1998a). *Schools and Volunteers: a Good Practice Guide to Using Volunteers After School.* London: Education Extra.

As the title implies, this is a practical guide for schools wishing to involve volunteers (including parents and older pupils) in study support activities. The book draws on a survey of schools to outline the potential role of volunteers, how to recruit them, supervision and training, payment and expenses. It provides numerous examples of how schools have used volunteers, and offers a guide to good practice together with a list of contact organisations.

(See also TOPPING, K. (1995), listed under the section on Literacy, above.)

Study support and homework

EDUCATION EXTRA (1998b). *Succeeding at Study Support: an Evaluation of 12 Model Projects in Primary and Secondary Schools.* London: Education Extra.

This short report presents case studies of 12 curriculum extension and homework projects. The case studies were designed to show what schools could do in a short time and with relatively modest resources. There are four primary school projects (two computer clubs, a mathematics club and a library/reading project). Common themes are drawn together to offer practical guidance on addressing key issues and ensuring the conditions for success.

GREAT BRITAIN. DEPARTMENT FOR EDUCATION AND EMPLOYMENT (1998a). *Extending Opportunity: a National Framework for Study Support.* London: DfEE.

This report defines study support as: 'learning activity outside normal school lessons which young people take part in voluntarily'. It offers a national framework for encouraging study support, involving: central government; LEAs; careers, library and youth services; business; and voluntary organisations and community groups. The report provides examples of how these agencies can help schools to provide study support, and highlights features of successful schemes. There is a set of answers to practical questions and a list of useful contacts and publications.

GREAT BRITAIN. DEPARTMENT FOR EDUCATION AND EMPLOYMENT (1998b). *Homework: Guidelines for Primary and Secondary Schools.* London: DfEE.

The Government is committed to the value of regular homework in schools. This report sets out guidelines on the purpose, type and amount of homework for children of different ages. There is advice on implementing the guidelines through whole school policies and home–school agreements. The report draws on research conducted by OFSTED and is illustrated by case-study examples.

WESTON, P. (1999). *Homework: Learning from Practice.* London: The Stationery Office.

The intention of this report is to be of direct use to schools in interpreting the Government's guidelines on homework. The report presents the findings from research specially commissioned for this purpose as well as drawing on the findings of previous research. It looks in detail at the purpose and scope of homework, the ways in which it can be made more effective, school policies and the impact of homework on pupils and parents.

Books and Articles Referred to in the Text

BOSSERT, S.T. (1988). 'Cooperative activities in the classroom.' In: ROTHKOPF, E.Z. (Ed) *Review of Research in Education* 15: 1988-89. Washington, DC: American Educational Research Association.

BROOKS, G., FLANAGAN, N., HENKHUZENS, Z. and HUTCHISON, D. (1998). *What Works for Slow Readers? The Effectiveness of Early Intervention Schemes.* Slough: NFER.

BROOKS, R., SUKHNANDAN, L. and SHARP, C. (1998). 'What are schools doing to raise achievement at KS2?' *Education Journal*, **21**, 28-9.

GILLBORN, D. and GIPPS, C. (1996). *Recent Research on the Achievements of Ethnic Minority Pupils* (OFSTED Reviews of Research). London: HMSO.

GREAT BRITAIN. DEPARTMENT FOR EDUCATION AND EMPLOYMENT (1997). *Blunkett Sets Tough New Targets* (Press Notice 96/97). London: DfEE.

GREAT BRITAIN. DEPARTMENT FOR EDUCATION AND EMPLOYMENT (1998). *Extending Opportunity: a National Framework for Study Support.* London: DfEE.

GREAT BRITAIN. DEPARTMENT FOR EDUCATION AND EMPLOYMENT. STANDARDS AND EFFECTIVENESS UNIT (1998). *Homework: Guidelines for Primary and Secondary Schools.* London: DfEE.

GREAT BRITAIN. WELSH OFFICE (1998). *National Curriculum Assessment Results in Wales: 1998. Key Stage 2.* Cardiff: Welsh Office, Education Department.

HARLEN, W. and MALCOLM, H. (1997). *Setting and Streaming: a Review of Research* (Using Research Series 18). Edinburgh: SCRE.

HARRIS, S., KEYS, W. and FERNANDES, C. (1997). *Third International Mathematics and Science Study, Second National Report. Part 1: Achievement in Mathematics and Science at Age 9 in England.* Slough: NFER.

JOHNSON, D.W. and JOHNSON, R.T. (1994). 'Collaborative learning and argumentation.' In: KUTNICK, P. and ROGERS C. (Eds) *Groups in Schools.* London: Cassell.

MacDONALD, A., SAUNDERS, L. and BENEFIELD, P. (1999). *Boys' Achievement, Progress, Motivation and Participation: Issues Raised by the Recent Literature.* Slough: NFER.

NUMERACY TASK FORCE (1998). *The Implementation of the National Numeracy Strategy: the Final Report of the Numeracy Task Force.* London: DfEE.

OFFICE FOR STANDARDS IN EDUCATION (1997). *Teachers Count* [Video]. London: OFSTED.

OFFICE FOR STANDARDS IN EDUCATION (1998a). *The Annual Report of Her Majesty's Chief Inspector of Schools: Standards and Quality in Education 1996/97.* London: OFSTED.

OFFICE FOR STANDARDS IN EDUCATION (1998b). *Setting in Primary Schools.* London: OFSTED.

OFFICE FOR STANDARDS IN EDUCATION (1998c). *Standards in the Primary Curriculum 1996-97.* London: OFSTED.

OFFICE FOR STANDARDS IN EDUCATION (1999a). *The Annual Report of Her Majesty's Chief Inspector of Schools: Standards and Quality in Education 1997/98.* London: OFSTED.

OFFICE FOR STANDARDS IN EDUCATION (1999b). R*aising the Attainment of Minority Ethnic Pupils: School and LEA Responses.* London: OFSTED.

QUALIFICATIONS AND CURRICULUM AUTHORITY (1998a). *Qualifying for Success: Report on the Consultation about the Future of Post-16 Qualifications.* London: QCA.

QUALIFICATIONS AND CURRICULUM AUTHORITY (1998b). *Standards at Key Stage 2: English, Mathematics and Science. Report on the 1998 National Curriculum Assessments for 11-year-olds. A Report for Headteachers, Teachers and Assessment Coordinators.* London: QCA.

REYNOLDS, D. and MUIJS, D. (1999). *National Numeracy Strategy: an Annotated Bibliography for Teachers and Schools.* London: DfEE, Standards and Effectiveness Unit.

SCHOOL CURRICULUM AND ASSESSMENT AUTHORITY (1997). *Expectations in Information Technology at Key Stages 1 and 2.* London: SCAA.

TOPPING, K. (1995). *Paired Reading, Spelling and Writing: the Handbook for Teachers and Parents.* London: Cassell.

TOPPING, K. and WHITELEY, M. (1993). 'Sex differences in the effectiveness of peer tutoring', *School Psychology International*, **14**, 1, 57-67.

WEINDLING, D. (1999). 'Kissing the frog: moving from school effectiveness to school improvement', *TOPIC*, Issue 21, Item 2.

Appendix

ABOUT THE RESEARCH

This book is based on research into strategies used by schools to raise achievement at Key Stage 2. The work was carried out in 1997/98 by a team of researchers at the National Foundation for Educational Research. The research formed part of the NFER's *Membership Programme*, which is funded by the Local Education Authorities in England and Wales.

The sample

In order to discover how schools were attempting to raise achievement at KS2, the research team contacted the LEA primary advisers throughout England and Wales, asking them to nominate up to three schools that had specific strategies in place to raise achievement at Key Stage 2. We received positive replies from 100 (64 per cent) of the LEAs. (At the time, many LEAs were involved in the local government reorganisation which led to the formation of new unitary authorities, and were therefore unable to respond to our request for information.) Altogether the advisers nominated a total of 245 schools.

Table 1: Summary of LEA contacts and response rate

Provided nominations of schools	100	64%
Declined to participate	20	13%
No response	37	23%
Total	**157**	**100%**

We contacted the heads of the nominated schools by telephone to obtain some brief details about their strategies. We entered all of the information on to a database so that we were able to gain an overview of: the different types of strategies that had been adopted; the rationale behind the adoption of the strategies; and the ways in which they were being monitored and evaluated. We also obtained some basic information about the characteristics of the schools. Further information about the strategies adopted by these schools is given in an article published in *Educational Journal* (Brooks *et al.*, 1998).

From the database we selected 12 schools as case studies. The selection of these schools was based on the following set of criteria, which was developed by the project team following discussions with our advisory group.

- That the heads felt their adopted strategies had *impacted positively on levels of achievement.*

- That our final sample included schools that had adopted strategies that *targeted behaviour/self-esteem*, as well as academic achievement.

- That some of the schools had implemented strategies for *all years within KS2* and others had implemented strategies that targeted *specific year groups within KS2.*

- That we included schools with strategies targeted at *specific groups of pupils* (e.g. boys, higher attaining pupils).

- That the schools served *a range of populations* in terms of geographical location, social deprivation and ethnic diversity.

School visits

We arranged to visit all 12 schools during the Autumn or Spring term of 1997/98. The visits were carried out by one or two researchers and lasted for about two days. During our visits we arranged to observe the strategies in practice and we held interviews with the headteacher, project coordinator, class teachers and pupils. In some cases, we also interviewed other people involved in the initiative, such as parents, volunteers, school governors and LEA advisers. We collected relevant documents, including evaluation reports, sample materials, lesson plans, school development plans, and OFSTED inspection reports.

The information obtained from the interviews, observations and documents was analysed and used to write a report on each of the case study schools. The draft manuscript was sent to the advisory group, internal readers, teachers and LEA advisers for comment.

Once the manuscript had been edited and re-drafted in the light of the readers' comments, the case-study reports were returned to each of the schools so that heads and class teachers could check them for factual accuracy. This gave us the opportunity to clarify any points with the schools and for them to let us know of any further developments that had taken place since our visit. The reports were amended to take account of the comments from schools.

Reference

BROOKS, R., SUKHNANDAN, L. and SHARP, C. (1998). 'What are schools doing to raise achievement at KS2?' *Education Journal*, **21**, 28-9.

THE CASE-STUDY SCHOOLS

Adderley Junior and Infants School, Birmingham
Alexandra Junior School, Stoke-on-Trent
Bawdsey Primary School, Suffolk
Berkeley Primary School, Gloucestershire
Carlton Junior and Infants School, Barnsley
Dorchester Road Primary School, Kingston upon Hull
Lord Deramore's Primary School, York
Mary Trevelyan Primary School, Newcastle upon Tyne
St Michael's Primary School, Doncaster
St Phillip Evans Primary School, Cardiff
Summerbee Junior School, Bournemouth
Whitcliffe Road Junior, Infants and Nursery School, Kirklees

THE PROJECT ADVISORY GROUP

Dr Judy Bradley, National Foundation for Educational Research
Ms Alix Beleschenko, Qualifications and Curriculum Authority
Ms Sheila Dainton, Association of Teachers and Lecturers
Mrs Roz Lamb, Norwood Green Primary School
Ms Janice Staines, British Educational Communications and Technology Agency
Mr Roy Storrs, HMI
Mr John Wilkinson, Hampshire Education Department

PEOPLE WHO COMMENTED ON THE FIRST DRAFT OF THE BOOK

Mr P.M. Booth, Westwood Farm Junior School
Mrs G. Coffey, Lynch Hill JMI School
Mrs A. Nicholls, NFER
Mr L. Prince, Belmont Middle School
Mrs C. Rawlings, Sheffield LEA
Mr G. Rees, Barn Street Junior School
Dr M. Sainsbury, NFER
Mr R. Wild, Yohden Primary School

Index